IN THE BLINK OF AN EYE

IN THE BLINK OF AN EYE

DALE, DAYTONA, AND THE DAY THAT CHANGED EVERYTHING

MICHAEL WALTRIP
AND ELLIS HENICAN

HYPERION
NEW YORK

Library of Congress Cataloging-in-Publication Data has been applied for.

ISBN: 978-1-4013-2431-5

Hyperion books are available for special promotions and premiums. For details contact the HarperCollins Special Markets Department in the New York office at 212-207-7528, fax 212-207-7222, or e-mail spsales@harpercollins.com.

Book design by Renato Stanisic

FIRST EDITION

10 9 8 7 6 5

THIS LABEL APPLIES TO TEXT STOCK

We try to produce the most beautiful books possible, and we are also extremely concerned about the impact of our manufacturing process on the forests of the world and the environment as a whole. Accordingly, we've made sure that all of the paper we use has been certified as coming from forests that are managed, to ensure the protection of the people and wildlife dependent upon them.

FOR MY HEROES:

If not for Darrell, I never would have started dreaming.
If not for Richard, I might still be dreaming.
If not for Dale, I don't believe my dreams
would have ever come true.

CONTENTS

IN THE BLINK OF AN EYE

INTRODUCTION

It was the four hundred and sixty-third time I had heard the National Anthem before a NASCAR Cup race. But somehow the song sounded different that day.

More hopeful. More heartfelt. Loaded with emotion, optimism, and opportunity.

O! say can you see by the dawn's early light
What so proudly we hailed at the twilight's last gleaming,

"Who are those boys up there singing?" I wondered. "O-Town? Yeah, I've heard of them." But they weren't the reason the song sounded special to me. It was where I was and what I knew could happen there: the Daytona International Speedway, February 18, 2001, a beautiful Sunday afternoon, opening day of my most anticipated NASCAR season ever.

Whose broad stripes and bright stars through the perilous fight,
O'er the ramparts we watched, were so were gallantly streaming?

As the song continued, I thought: I love this racetrack. I love its high-banked turns and the tight racing action. Daytona was the perfect track to me. Running in the draft was what I did best. Being in Daytona always made me feel like a kid again. From the first time I laid eyes on that amazing track as an eleven-year-old boy, it had always felt like home to me.

And there I stood beside my new ride, the #15 NAPA car, a car I knew I could win in. My crew was behind me. My confidence was solid. My karma was balanced, whatever karma is. I'd heard people use that expression before. I was surrounded by many of the people I loved: my wife, Buffy. My daughters, Caitlin and Macy. A whole bunch of other family and friends. They were all at the track that Sunday. They believed in me. They always had. All of us sensed this day could be something we would never forget.

This was my first race with my new team. Not just any team, either. I had joined Dale Earnhardt, Inc. My new boss was one of NASCAR's greatest drivers ever. He was also proving to be a brilliant team owner. Dale built winners. His teams had won championships in NASCAR, first in the truck series and then, with his son Dale Junior driving, in the Busch series too. After those championships, Dale turned his team's focus to Cup racing, where the big boys play. He was already winning there.

As I looked up ahead of me on the grid, I saw Dale standing beside his famous black #3 Chevy. I felt so lucky to be on his team. I was driving for the Man. "The Intimidator," race fans called him. He was wildly aggressive and fiercely competitive. His driving style defined what our sport was all about. Dale had won seven NASCAR Cup championships. He and Richard Petty were tied with the most. The previous season, Dale had almost gotten his eighth. Pushing fifty, he still had it.

Dale and I had shared a lot of good times together. He was my friend.

And the rockets' red glare, the bombs bursting in air,

As the O-Town boys made their way through the hard-to-sing part, my mind was wandering all over the place: "How did they get this gig? Wouldn't Hank Junior be more NASCAR? Aw, look at that." I could see Dale up there putting his arm around Teresa, his wife. Smooth move, Dale, I thought. I put my arm around Buffy. Dale was my mentor, after all, and my racing coach and my hang-out-and-go-fishin' buddy—and now, he was my car owner too. That meant he would be an ally on the track. Man, that sounded great! The guy who racers dreaded seeing in their mirror was now my partner and my boss. Just two days earlier, he had explained to me how we were going to win the Daytona 500. That was amazing. But I'll tell you more about that later.

Ever since I was a kid, Daytona was where I wanted to be in February. NASCAR kicked off every year with a bang, the Super Bowl of stock-car racing. That meant my first race on Dale's team would be the forty-third running of the Great American Race, the Daytona 500.

Winning the 500 is every NASCAR racer's dream. To join the list of names inscribed on the Harley J. Earl trophy makes you part of the sport's elite. Richard Petty's name is on there seven times. Dale is there too, along with my brother Darrell. So are David Pearson, Jeff Gordon, Jimmie Johnson, Bobby Allison, Cale Yarborough, and Mario Andretti. And that's just some of them. I fantasized about my name being on there with the greats. I certainly wasn't shy about dreaming large, was I?

Gave proof through the night that our flag was still there.

"Oh, I get it," I said to myself. "O-Town, Orlando. They live close by. Hank's all the way up in Tennessee. Guess he didn't want to make the trip down."

Going into this race, I had been on quite a roll. A bad roll. Do I know a bad roll when I'm stuck on one? Yes, I think I do. This roll was four hundred and sixty-two NASCAR Cup losses long, without a single win. That's right, 0–462.

There. I said it.

All those losses: That was always the pink elephant in most any room I was in.

Four hundred and sixty-two times in a row, I had started my engine in a NASCAR Cup race and taken a green flag. When the checkered flag flew and I pulled in and shut my engine off, there was not a trophy queen in sight. No confetti flying. No champagne corks in the air. I had become very familiar with the look of long faces after long races.

In the previous fifty-three years of NASCAR history, no one had ever lost that many races in a row—and then won one. All drivers lose more than they win. Even the King, Richard Petty. He got beat over eight hundred times. Of course, he also won a record two hundred races along the way. You do the math. That's about one in every five starts the King would win. I think that puts my 0–462 into perspective, don't you?

I wondered why all that losing wasn't bothering me that day. Because it didn't bother Dale, I guess. He hired me and told me I'd win in his car. And I believed him.

O! say does that star-spangled banner yet wave

I was thinking about all that and a whole lot more as I stood with my hand on my heart. My head was crowded with all kinds of junk that didn't matter. I was glad it was almost time to climb into my car. When I got in there, nothing but racing would be getting in with me. But for a little while longer, my mind was shooting everywhere. I sure was missing my dad. He had always been in Daytona with me. He would have been so happy seeing me all suited up and ready to go racing for Dale.

It sure felt weird that Darrell wasn't racing with me this time. It was my first 500 without him on the track with me. But he'd be watching from way up top. It was his first day on his new job, calling the action for Fox television. My momma was going to love this, I thought. I could picture her back in North Carolina in front of that big TV I bought her, listening to DW talk about his little brother while the whole world watched with her.

O'er the land of the free and the home of the brave?

What happened after those boys stopped singing would ultimately change my life. If you're thinking, "Oh, what a sweet story! Michael Waltrip finally wins a race!"—you're right. I did. But there was so much more to it than that. In the blink of an eye, everything changed. And not just for me. Many people's lives would never be the same. Racing wouldn't. NASCAR wouldn't. Millions of people around the world would feel like something important had been snatched from them— and it would have been.

Up until now, I haven't talked much about that day in Daytona. And I know the story better than anyone. For ten years, I did everything I could to avoid focusing on it at all. I didn't want to go there. It was too painful. The memories hurt too much. And besides, I didn't understand what some parts of the story meant. It was too deep for me. When people asked, I would change the subject. If they persisted, I would leave the room. For years, my strategy was just to squish it down and keep it there. Any psychologist would say that's a bad strategy, but I thought I could make it work for me. Never once, until recently, had I even watched the TV coverage or a video of the race. I certainly knew the outcome, and I didn't want to relive it.

But nobody lived that day like I did. Nobody could tell the story like I could. I felt like I owed that to the people who were still hurting. Every year they return to Daytona and feel that pain again.

I want to help those people. I want to tell them some Dale stories I bet they've never heard before, some stories that will make them smile. People loved the Intimidator. They'll love the Dale I knew even more.

Like any important story of triumph and tragedy, this one didn't start on the day of its shocking climax. It didn't end that day either. The story started decades earlier in a small town in western Kentucky. The story continues today.

For many years, people in the racing world have known me as a sponsor-endorsing, TV-talking, commercial-making, fan-friendly race-car driver, a guy who loves his family and loves what he got to do. They might mention that I had a few losses on the track along the way.

But of all those losses, there's only one I think about every day.

When I decided to tell this story, my deepest hope was that it would bring comfort to others. What I found is that it's brought relief to me.

Dale made me a winner that day in Daytona. He continues to do that today. You will see what I mean as you read my story. I'm so glad I am finally able to open up and share it with you.

PART 1:
DREAMING

CHAPTER 1

EARLY YEARS

I love sports. When I was a kid, I played them all. You couldn't find a boy in Owensboro, Kentucky, in the 1970s who played as many sports as I did, and played them with as much mediocrity. Football, baseball, basketball, tennis. I was amazingly average at them all.

If there were twenty players on a team, I'd be chosen no better than twelfth every time. I once told one of my coaches I thought I might try to play some college ball. His reaction? "We have a very good shop program here at Burns Middle School. Maybe you should start looking into that."

That coach was also the guidance counselor. His guidance led me to think I probably wouldn't be running, throwing, jumping, or tackling my way to a college scholarship. I actually could have been a pretty good tackler, I think, if I could have just caught someone.

As I considered my options, I realized something extremely important: Chances were, when I grew up I'd have to make a living sitting on my butt. And looking around town, it seemed like everyone who had a sit-down job had gotten good grades in school. Unfortunately, I wasn't that guy either.

What did that leave? I could drive a cab, I figured, but we didn't have any of those in Owensboro. I could be a security guard, but nobody ever stole much in our town.

I knew one guy who got to make a living sitting down, and his job looked like a whole lot of fun to me. From what I could tell, it paid well too. This guy had figured it out. From what I'd heard, he was no better in the classroom than I was.

. . . .

My mom and dad, Margaret and Leroy, had five children. I was the baby. Darrell was the oldest. When I came along, he was sixteen and already making a name for himself sitting down in a car, driving fast and winning races.

The idea sounded perfect. You sit on your butt to drive a race car. How 'bout that? That was it. I made up my mind. I wanted to be a race-car driver. Just like my brother was. My little-kid logic was solid, don't you think?

When I was born, our family of seven was living in a three-bedroom house on the west end of town. Mom had a part-time job as a cashier at the IGA grocery store. Dad worked at the Pepsi plant. Despite them working all day and raising us kids, we had a pretty regular routine. Mom served dinner in our kitchen every night at six, and Dad made sure we had the nicest yard on our street.

Supporting a family with five children was tough. Yet my parents always found ways to give us kids whatever we needed. Needed, I said. Not wanted. I found it very difficult back then to understand the difference between needing and wanting. I felt like if I wanted something really badly—well, then I must need it.

My perspective resulted in some lively debates between me and my parents. I mostly lost, but I wasn't shy about letting them know where I stood. Some of my opinions resulted in some pretty tough love. I certainly got my share of whippings, as most kids did back then. That's how my parents were raised. That's how they raised us. My own girls should consider themselves lucky I didn't elect to continue that tradition.

Growing up, I was a busy, emotional, funny kid. My parents tried to teach me discipline and responsibility. I would say they had partial success. But I came away with something from my childhood I've always liked about myself: the way I respect and appreciate people. That's how my parents treated everyone. As an adult, that's how I've always tried to treat people too. I'm a reflection of my parents, and I've wanted to make them proud.

My birth was an accident. Not so much the birth part, but the conception part. I came into the family late. But if you ask Mom today, she'll say all five of us were accidents. Darrell told me it was embarrassing for him when Mom would come to get him at a track meet or some school function while she was all pregnant with me. None of the other high-school kids' moms were expecting.

When I came along, at least for a little while, Mom and Dad must have been like, "I thought we were done with all this kid-raising stuff. And now we got one more to deal with?"

I say that because there is very limited evidence that I existed until I was four or five years old. No baby pictures. My binky and my blankie— where's all that stuff? I never found it anywhere, not even in the box in the attic.

You can imagine how crowded it was in our little house. Seven people, three bedrooms, one bath. But Darrell moved out quickly. With Dad working full-time and Mom part-time, my older sister Carolyn was left in charge of me a lot. I called Carolyn "Mom," which certainly didn't help her dating life.

"You got a kid?" guys would ask her. "That little boy just said, 'Come here, Momma.'"

Even after Darrell and Carolyn left home, there were still five of us in the house: Mom and Dad, plus me, my brother Bobby, and my sister Connie. Poor Connie grew up with a roommate: me. We shared a room until I was nine or ten. Connie could not wait for Bobby to move out so she could get rid of me and finally have her own room.

Bobby had an Afro and would spend an unusual amount of time in the bathroom before school fixing his hair. Connie had hair too, and she certainly needed to get ready for school. But Bobby was the oldest still at home, and he pretty much ran the show—for sure when Mom and Dad weren't around.

I've always wondered if being an "accident" and taking orders from Darrell, Carolyn, Bobby, Connie, Mom, and Dad had anything to do with my lifelong need to prove myself. I don't know. But I sure got tired of taking orders from all those people—and their friends too.

My mom was devoted to all her children. But by the time she was down to the fifth one, she wasn't all that lovey-dovey anymore. Her favorite saying was, "You'll live."

Fall down, skin your knee raw? You'll live.

Didn't make the baseball team? You'll live.

Girlfriend dumped you? You'll live. Whatever happened, you'll live.

Today if I say to my little girl, Macy, "You'll live," we laugh. She knows that's our little joke about her grandma.

My mom is funny. She has a very quick wit. So being around her sometimes was cool. Since Mom worked only part-time, mostly I hung out with her. I'd go just about everywhere she did. We used to ride to my aunt's to visit once a month or so. Aunt Emma lived in the little town of Henderson, Kentucky, about a half hour away.

One particular day, I wasn't too happy about making the trip. I didn't want to go at all. And I whined all the way to Henderson.

My friends were having a big bicycle race that day, and I was missing it. On the way back, I told my mom she had ruined my whole day. Mom reminds me of that even now and says that I was being a little bit dramatic. That could be true. When we spend time together these days and I get ready to leave, Mom will still sometimes say: "See you soon. Don't let anybody ruin your day." We get a good laugh out of that one.

I always admired the way my mom loved, respected, and supported Dad. I mean, life wasn't easy for either of them. Her role in the family— working a job, being home to take care of us, cooking, cleaning—was tough. I appreciated the strength of character she had. I don't think her day-to-day life was much fun back then. But she always found ways to give each of us the attention we craved.

Dad was working hard and climbing the ladder at Pepsi. He'd get to the plant at five-thirty in the morning to make sure all the trucks were loaded up and ready to go. By the time he got home at six each night he was pretty well worn out. There wasn't any playing pitch and catch with him in the evenings. He was about done for the day.

After working all week, Dad looked forward to the weekend. Sometimes those weekends included going off to the races with Darrell. I was just a little boy when Darrell started racing in NASCAR. So I never got to make any of those guy trips. I'd be stuck at home with Momma.

Man, that killed me!

I wanted to be at the races too. I didn't understand that I was just a kid and didn't belong on the road with the guys. I was already a huge fan of the sport. Or as much of one as I could be, considering my favorite sport wasn't on TV hardly at all. Occasionally, you could catch a few laps of NASCAR action on ABC's *Wide World of Sports*. They would squeeze a race in between sumo wrestling and the World Ping-Pong

Championships. But that was about it. And as you kids may have heard, we didn't have the Internet back then.

But I did get to go to the races some. And what I saw there made me fall in love with NASCAR.

We used to get *Stock Car Racing* magazine delivered to the house every month. As soon as Dad was done reading, he would let me have the magazine. I couldn't wait to get my hands on it. Every month, there was a poster of a driver and his car in the center of the magazine. I pulled those posters out and hung them on my wall. All of them. Richard Petty, David Pearson, the Allisons, Cale Yarborough. There was even one of my hero, my brother Darrell. But I was mostly only able to see DW race on the local track. What I wanted more than anything was to see my brother racing against the stars of NASCAR.

With Dad off at the races and Mom knowing how badly I wanted to be there too, she cut a deal with me. If I didn't complain too much about being stuck at home with her, she would take me to listen to the races on the radio. Like I said, back in the seventies there wasn't a whole lot of NASCAR racing on TV. But there was one way for us to follow how Darrell was doing. A radio station in Clarksville, Tennessee, carried the races every weekend. We couldn't pick it up in Owensboro. So Mom and I would get in the car and drive down the road toward Tennessee. When we could pick up the signal from that station, we'd pull over and listen to the race.

Can you imagine? Driving an hour so we could listen to a race on the radio? With your mom? Things have changed quite dramatically since then. If I told Macy that's what we were going to do one Sunday afternoon, she would be like, "Yeah, right, Dad." But I thought it was so cool. Mom knew how much that meant to me. And other than a little gas, it was probably a cheap way to entertain a little kid on a Sunday afternoon.

One of the first things I recall doing with my dad, just him and me, was on Sunday mornings when I was eleven or twelve. We didn't go to church much. But Dad and I started going to McDonald's. When we first began doing that, we'd each get an Egg McMuffin. And when we were finished, we'd both still be hungry. So Dad got us each another one. We both ate the second one, but that was too much. So we started ordering just three—one for each of us and we'd split the third one. Dad would cut it right down the middle with a plastic Mickey D's knife.

That may not sound like much. They were just Egg McMuffins. But those Sunday-morning breakfasts were the first thing I remember that my dad and I ever shared.

He seemed to like it too. Those trips to McDonald's became a Sunday-morning ritual for the two of us.

God bless Ronald and that aggravating Hamburglar too! We were sharing more than a breakfast sandwich. We were sharing stories about my life. We'd talk about school and racing and just normal stuff. For some reason, we never talked about girls, though. A wife and two kids later, I'm still waiting for the birds-and-bees story to be told to me.

But for the first time, I felt a real connection with my dad. I was growing up. We found some things in common. He was noticing me. And I loved the attention.

CHAPTER 2

HEADED SOUTH

I was like most little kids in this way: I hated getting up in the morning. Most every day of the week was about the same. Up crazy early. Fight for time in the bathroom. Head out the door with a crappy attitude, destined for another boring day of school. I didn't know much, but I knew one thing. I didn't like any of that routine. Those days always seemed to go from bad to worse.

But one Wednesday was different from all the other days of the year. It came in mid-February. That Wednesday, I couldn't wait to get the day started. Instead of me chasing the number 10 bus down Greenbriar Street, I was out at the corner in plenty of time, the first one there.

The sooner I was on the bus, the sooner the school day would start and the sooner lunchtime would arrive. That's how I had it figured. On that particular Wednesday, I wouldn't be staring at a plastic lunch tray with mystery meat and two sides in the Stanley Elementary School cafeteria. I'd be looking for Mom and Dad in the hallway outside my classroom, our four-door Chevy Caprice Classic loaded and idling at the curb out front.

When the lunch bell rang, Mom and Dad were there and ready to go. "I'll bring y'all back some pictures of the cars," I'd tell the other kids. With that, I was down the hall and out the door. We jumped in the car and took off toward Daytona Beach, Florida.

Forget the fact that I was getting out of school for a few days. It was where we were going that was the best part. We were heading to the Daytona 500, the annual kickoff to the NASCAR season, what I considered to be heaven on earth. And us Waltrips weren't your average, ordinary fans. One of us was in the race. Not only was my brother DW competing, he would be contending too.

It was about a twelve-hour drive south from Owensboro to racing's holy land. Dad would drive straight through the night. The ride was a bit of a challenge for a little kid, to say the least. We listened to whatever Dad wanted to hear on the radio, and he smoked a lot. Heck, Mom would smoke too, and she didn't even smoke. I guess she thought, "If you can't beat 'em . . ." I just rode in the back and complained. A lot.

What else did I have to do? I didn't have anybody to play with. My brothers and sisters didn't make this trip. It was just me in the back. And man, did my parents get on my nerves. It was cold outside and Dad would rarely crack a window. With all the smoke, I could barely see where we were going. About the time he would finish one cigarette, he'd light up another.

And he had this Roy Clark 8-track tape that I hated. At first. The more I heard it, the more it grew on me. There was one particular song I loved to hear. It was called "I Never Picked Cotton."

I never picked cotton,
But my mother did and my brother did

Sorry. I digress. Hope you enjoyed that sweet Roy Clark tune.

Anything to pass the time on a smoky ride to Daytona. You know it was a long way down there if I memorized the lyrics to Roy's cotton-picking song. And I haven't forgotten them yet.

Dad was a trouper though. Between his cigarettes and coffee, he never needed to rest. With just one stop for gas, eating the sandwiches Momma packed, we made really good time. We hit Daytona early Thursday morning, checked into the hotel, and got a couple of hours of sleep. By seven A.M. we were heading downstairs for breakfast.

By the time we sat down for some bacon and eggs, I could already feel it. Daytona was NASCAR. This town was all about racing.

The *Daytona Beach News-Journal* was full of articles about the 500 and full-color photos of the racing action and the drivers. Pictures of race cars in a newspaper! How cool was that? Back home there was never a picture of a race car in our newspaper. I only got that once a month when Dad's magazine would show up.

And Thursday was the best day to get to town. Speedweek was wide open. The cars had been on the track for a few days by then. They'd be lined up and ready for the qualifying races that afternoon. Dad never wanted to miss the twin 125-mile qualifying races, and I didn't either. He would always say those races were the best ones of the week.

After we got done eating, it was time to head to the racetrack, my favorite place to be. That long, smoke-filled drive on Wednesday didn't matter anymore. In fact, it was totally worth it. Plus that ride was probably the reason I never started smoking, which is a bonus.

It's interesting, looking back to those races in the mid-1970s. I was just a kid who loved cars. Loved being in Daytona, dreaming of racing on those famous high banks one day. Not only racing on them but winning on them. Back then, I was already dreaming of being out there.

One thing was obvious: You can't race if you don't qualify. That made sense to me. And you could tell by the way those boys raced on Thursday, it made sense to them too. These races were exciting and action-packed. That made them fan favorites. But they also were pressure cookers for the teams and the drivers.

It was about a fifteen-minute ride from the hotel to the racetrack. And the whole way, I thought about driving through Daytona's famous tunnel. To get to the Speedway infield, you had to go through a tunnel that went under turn four. To me, that tunnel separated this special place from all that was going on in the real world. I was a boy separated from racing until I went through that tunnel. When I got through there, I would be right where I wanted to be.

Outside the tunnel is where most of the fans were, up in the grandstand. There were some through the tunnel. They had their campers there and were enjoying the Daytona experience. They were tailgating. But I don't think we called it that back then. I wasn't stopping in the infield. But I was heading toward the pit area. I remember thinking, I'm driving through the same tunnel Richard Petty had driven through. And when I popped out the other side, there they were, those famous Daytona high banks. They were so cool to me. I was fascinated by them. Most kids didn't get it. I tried to explain the Daytona turns to my friends. They just looked at me funny. I would say, "They're special turns, y'all." I'd tell them those turns were so steep and tall, I didn't even see how a car could stay up there.

That was probably a pretty smart thing for a kid to question. I am still amazed about that place even today. I can't imagine the faces of people when Bill France, who built Daytona, said, "I'm going to bank the turns at thirty-one degrees. They're gonna be about three stories tall."

Someone check his temperature, I'm sure people thought.

There wasn't another place like Daytona in the whole world. The vision that man had to have in order to build something so massive, so unique, so ahead of his time, is just incredible. It's incomprehensible to me still. He was a genius. The track opened in 1959 and is still the world center of racing today. I bet Mr. France would tell people back then, "Check out the turns. Walk up the banks if you want. But you'll need to take your shoes off."

Or how would you like to have been the dude running the paving machine? He probably said, "You want me to do what?"

It was enough to send my mind into overdrive. Because things were about to get even better. As much as I loved looking at the track, seeing those cars race around the high banks really took my breath away.

So fast, so close to each other—what a thrill!

And right there in the middle of all that action was my brother Darrell, doing exactly what I'd decided I wanted to do.

CHAPTER 3

COOL BROTHER

I loved and admired my brother Darrell. I wanted to be just like him. I decided I was going to be a race-car driver too. I thought, "Man, he's living the dream! He is racing cars against Richard Petty. And that's all he does. That's his job. How cool would that be?" That's all I thought about. I wanted to do just what my brother was doing. And I was ready to start.

When Darrell was about my age, late eleven or early twelve, he started racing go-karts. That's what I needed to do. The first step was getting my hands on one of those babies.

Getting started racing was going to be tough for me. It took money to race, even go-karts, and I didn't have any to speak of. I mowed yards and babysat my niece and nephew some. But like most kids, I spent that money on candy or going to the arcade. So I needed some help. Actually, a lot of help.

It looked to me like Darrell had plenty of money. He could help. When Darrell and his wife, Stevie, would come back to Kentucky, which wasn't very often, they always had a new car. And Darrell was a sharp dresser. Plus, Stevie's parents were rich. We sort of lived on the opposite sides of town. And their end of town was much more, let's say, comfortable. Darrell and Stevie had left Owensboro and moved to Tennessee when they married so Darrell could be closer to the racing action. I didn't spend much time around him. No brotherly mentoring. No talks about girls or school or life. No playing ball in the schoolyard together.

We didn't have a relationship. I didn't get to know him until we were both adults.

One thing I did know quite well was Darrell's shadow. Darrell was about all anyone around town talked about. And at home too. His shadow had kept me mostly hidden from my dad. Or at least my desire to become a racer was hidden. He didn't pay any attention to how serious I was about getting my career started. Of course, I was eleven. Not many eleven-year-olds are serious about much.

But I was. I was determined to race. The only thing I had to race, though, was my bike. I used to convince all my friends that it would be fun to run a one-hundred-lap bike race around the playground instead of just a lap or two like most kids did. That was more like a drag race, not a NASCAR race. I had a Schwinn, and it was sweet! I remember racing that bike and wanting to win every time. But how was I going to get from that Schwinn to those high banks of Daytona? That's what I had to figure out.

Dilemma: Mom and Dad had heard me say repeatedly that I wanted to be a race-car driver. But they just shrugged it off. Their sentiment was, "Yeah, we know you do. So does every other kid in this town. They all want to do what your brother is doing. Get over it and go ride your bike."

Also, my problems getting a kart and going racing were more complicated than just a lack of cash. Who would work on the kart? I didn't know how to do that. Dad did, but he was working his butt off at Pepsi. And Mom's job at the grocery store was just to fill in the gaps between Dad's checks and all the bills that come in when you're raising a family. But at the time, I didn't really have a clue. I was just a kid. I used to tell Mom, "Just write a check. I know you have some. I saw 'em in your purse." Don't be looking in your mom's purse, kids. It'll just cause problems.

I just wanted to race. But how?

It looked like I was going to have to lob a call in to brother Darrell. I was fairly certain I knew how that would go, but I had to give it a try. I thought he would say no. I just hoped he wouldn't be mean to me about it and tell me to go ride my bike like my dad had. Maybe if Darrell wouldn't come up with the cash for the kart, he would at least come up with some direction how to get started. So I mustered up the courage to call Big Brother and see what I'd get for an answer. It wasn't easy. I hardly knew Darrell. And as I suspected, that call didn't go over very well with him.

"Hey, Darrell," I started. "Wouldn't it be cool if there was another Waltrip racing in NASCAR?"

"Uh," he said, "what do you want?"

"I want to be a race-car driver," I told him, a statement I'm sure Darrell had used many times when he was young and people asked about his dream. "I need a go-kart to get started. Can you help your little brother out?"

I used the little-brother reference to play to his sentimental side. Smart, huh? Then I continued: "Oh, and I will probably need some spare parts and some tires and other stuff too."

I can hear the words he used that day, close to forty years ago, as if he said them yesterday. "You're wasting your time, Mikey," he said. "You just don't understand how much road there is between Owensboro and Daytona."

He was wrong there. Actually, I did. I also understood clearly how many cigarettes Dad could smoke on that road.

Darrell was speaking figuratively, of course. But there was nothing figurative about his answer: no.

He continued: "All you're gonna do is waste a lot of your time and other people's money. You need to concentrate on school. Focus your energy on that. Making it in NASCAR is a one-in-a-million shot."

Huh? One in a million? So you're saying I got a shot?

But seriously, those were words no little kid wanted to hear from his hero about his dream.

I totally understand it today. It is such a huge commitment to own a race team. Believe me, I know. Even if you're just talking about a go-kart team. Plus, I'm sure Darrell knew Dad wouldn't want any part of this. He'd been through it all with Darrell and knew what a huge time-and-money suck racing was.

Way before I was born, when Dad had been promoted at the Pepsi plant and moved up from loading and driving trucks to route manager, Big Brother had convinced Dad to buy him a go-kart. Daddy was an accomplished shade-tree mechanic. Or a "jack of all trades, master of none," Dad would say. I'm sure DW convinced Dad it would be a lot of fun. Darrell also told Dad he would mow people's grass every day to help pay for the kart. Dad bought that story and then a go-kart—and DW was in business. Either Darrell was a better salesman than I was or yard-mowing paid a lot more back then. Hmm. But either way, they got a go-kart, and Darrell needed to learn how to drive it. So they hauled it to a big, empty parking lot there in town, and Darrell took off.

I wasn't around back then. But I saw pictures, and Dad was all in. Buying parts, tires, oil, gas—whatever it took to go racing. After Darrell learned how to drive his new kart around that parking lot, they were off to the races. And they won. A lot. They were racing all over the Midwest. It was all-consuming for everyone in the family. Mom, Dad, and the four kids. But especially for Dad.

By the time I got to the age where I wanted to try racing, Mom and Dad were getting a little older. Dad was in his fifties then. And I think the thought of working at Pepsi all day, then coming home and working on a go-kart half the night wasn't overly appealing to him. His and Mom's idea of fun on the weekends consisted of Friday and Saturday nights at the Moose Lodge and Sundays listening to or watching the races.

The rejection hurt me some then, for sure. But I loved my parents, and I always was thankful for both of them. Their not wanting to help me with my dream turned out to be a perfect motivation for me to go find other ways to get it done.

I think that's part of the fierce independence that makes me who I am today. That independence became a key ingredient of success in my career and my life. No matter what obstacles I faced, I always knew I could overcome them and succeed. You have to be creative when considering options or alternative plans. Most important, you can't ever give up. Luckily, I learned these lessons at a very young age. If you aren't already aware, you will find out as you read along that I got on a bit of a losing streak for a few years, one that I might not have been able to overcome had Mom and Dad just bought me a go-kart, or had Darrell just said, "Sure, whatever you need, Brother." To even get started in racing I had to be persistent. And later in life, one word that probably came to describe my career better than any other would be "persistent."

Now back to the problem of how I was going to get my shot at racing.

Mom and Dad, strike one.

Darrell, strike two.

So where should I swing next? Asking Mom and Dad and Darrell over and over would have been persistent, I guess, but not very creative. Besides, I tried that with Dad. And his nos just kept getting louder and louder.

How about my other brother, Bobby?

Bobby had recently moved from Owensboro down to Tennessee to go to work for Darrell. Darrell had started a race-car parts business and asked Bobby to manage it for him. Bobby also raced and even got a shot at stock cars at Kentucky Motor Speedway in Owensboro. But that didn't go so well, so he mostly just raced go-karts. I had mowed Bobby's grass and done odd jobs for him over the summer. I guess we sort of had a relationship, more than me and Darrell for sure. I went to bat one more time. I called up Bobby and told him I wanted to be a race-car driver. "Can I drive your go-kart, Bobby, and see how I do?"

"Yeah, sure, Bro," Bobby said.

He must not have understood the question, I thought.

"I was hoping you'd let me drive it," I said this time.

"Yeah, I get it," Bobby said. "You drive. Yes. Sure."

Well, darn! Finally, someone who understood me.

Woo-hoo! Let's go racing!

Then Bobby said, "There's a race down here Sunday. If you can get yourself here, you can race."

"Awesome! That is so cool. I will be there."

"You come down Saturday," he said. "We'll get you all fitted up in the kart."

Then he asked, "How you gonna get here?"

Hmmm . . . good question. I'm eleven—how'm I supposed to get there? I asked myself.

Then Bobby said, "If you can get to Bowling Green, I'll pick you up there."

"Deal," I said immediately. "I'll see you Saturday."

You know the old adage "It's better to laugh than to cry"? My daddy used to say that a lot. Well, that's what I was doing on Saturday morning. There I sat on a Greyhound bus, looking around, laughing at myself. Couldn't get anyone to take me to Bowling Green, which is about half-way to Nashville. But at least Mom was nice enough to give me a ride to the bus station.

In a car, it's an hour's drive from Owensboro to Bowling Green. By bus, it was almost three. We made stops in little towns that weren't even towns, I don't think. It took forever. But I didn't care. It was going to be worth it.

Then we pulled into the bus station in Bowling Green, and I wondered if Bobby would actually be there.

Robert Lynn (Bobby) Waltrip was in his mid-twenties, and he was a little crazy. So, as I peered out the window of the bus looking for Bob, I wasn't a hundred percent sure I'd actually find him. But as the bus rolled to a stop I saw my brother sliding around the corner, right on time. And, man, he had one of the coolest cars ever! It was a new Oldsmobile 442, maroon and gold.

I watched Bobby skid to a stop at the station. And I thought, Man, I got a cool brother. Look at that 'fro he's sporting. Look at those smooth wheels. But what made him the coolest to me was just that he was there. He had come through for me.

I'm positive there were at least a thousand other things my twenty-five-year-old brother could have been doing on a Saturday afternoon. Instead of doing any of those things, he came to get me. First, it was Dad with the McMuffins. Then it was Bob sharing the love in his 442. The mentoring was beginning just when I needed it.

CHAPTER 4

GAS RIGHT

Mikey got an upgrade. I went from an old Greyhound bus to a sporty new 442. Cool Bro and I were off to the races, rolling toward Nashville, Tennessee. I was excited. And as any young boy would have, I suppose, I wanted to impress Bobby right away with my extensive racing knowledge.

"I got this, Bob," I told him. "I know I can do it. I know what lines to take in the corners. I know how to swing out next to the wall on the straights. And then, when I win, I have to thank my sponsors in Victory Lane, just like Darrell does."

"Thank you, God, Goody's, and Goodyear," Darrell liked to say.

Then Bobby asked me something I hadn't thought of. "Do you know which side the gas pedal is on and which side's the brake?"

"Ah, yes, sir," I answered. "Well, no. Not exactly."

Thinking, thinking, thinking . . .

"I think right. But I get confused." I guess I was more like a virtual race-car driver. I'd never actually done it before. But I sure had seen it done plenty of times.

"Little brother, that ain't nothing like the real thing," Bobby said. He knew I needed real experience.

Bobby's shop was located just out of Nashville in Franklin, Tennessee. When we got there and checked out his kart, Bobby began to talk me through everything I had to know the next day when I got to the track. Even the basics were intimidating to me though. I was like a sponge, trying to soak up everything.

"Gas on right, brake on left," Bobby said. And I kept repeating that quietly to myself. "What if I forget that little detail?" I thought.

And things got even more complicated from there. I needed to know how to tune the engine on the track. What to listen for. What to do in order to make sure the engine was running right.

When I went to bed that night, I was so scared I couldn't sleep.

The next day was my big day, what I'd been dreaming of. I was totally excited to be there. But mostly scared. What if I wasn't good at this? There was no way to know if I would be. You can't tell by looking at a kid if he can drive or not. What if I messed something up? What if I wrecked? That would surely make Bobby mad. I knew it would. And that engine-tuning thing. I had to get that right. Bobby said if I didn't do it correctly, I would melt his engine down. That, I was sure, would be career-ending. Really? My career was ending? It hadn't even begun!

I was so worried about what I was getting ready to do, I was already thrown by even the simplest details, like what side the gas pedal was on. But I had a plan. I found a big, fat pen and I put a large G on my right tennis shoe and a B on my left.

Just in case.

When I woke up Sunday morning I laced up my marked sneakers, and off to the track we went. It was located in Smyrna, about twenty miles from Bobby's house. When I got there and checked out the track, it looked like it had about six turns. Bobby said I was going to race in the rookie junior class. When it was time to practice, I put on a leather jacket and a helmet that Bobby gave me and I hopped on his kart. Even with my brother coaching me, telling me everything to do, I was still really nervous about the thought of pulling onto the track for the first time. But as soon as I did, the nervousness went away, and my focus was directed on the Smyrna Speedway. Right off, I felt comfortable. It felt natural to me. I was doing what I'd seen DW do a zillion times. It was like I got it. And my first laps? They weren't great laps, but they were pretty good, I guess.

After practice, Bobby patted me on the back and said, "Good job, Little Bro."

"Really? You think I did good?" I asked him.

"You did great. I'm proud of you."

I was off to a promising start.

My brother was proud of me. Not the one I had put up on a pedestal my whole life. The other brother. The one who was there when I had two strikes against me and I was trying to figure out how I was going to go race. He gave me the chance, and I made him proud. I was feeling really good about this day.

When it was time for my race, I was ready. There were just four of us rookie kids. I think my kart was probably better than theirs. And I won. By a lot.

When I pulled in, they handed me the checkered flag and told me to take a victory lap. I thought to myself: "Yes! I love this. And I'm good at it. I knew I'd love it. I wasn't so sure I'd be good at it. But I was. I won." I couldn't believe it. This had to be as good as it got.

The first person I saw after the race was Bobby, and he had a huge smile on his face. He was a team owner, mechanic, and driver-coach, but mostly I could tell he was a proud big brother. The next person I saw was the trophy queen, holding my winning prize. Bobby told me I had to kiss her to get my trophy.

What? That scared me more than the thought of racing had that day.

Luckily for me, the queen and I decided we would just shake hands and call it even. That afternoon, on the way back to meet my bus, Bobby and I talked nonstop. Or maybe I talked nonstop and Bobby just listened. But I know one thing he said for sure. He said that by the end of my race, the lap times I was running were comparable to his. Really? I had watched Bobby win races before. Being as fast as him meant a lot to me. He may have just been saying that to be nice, I don't know. But it sure was a good thing to hear.

It was getting close to dark when we drove up to the bus station. Bobby hugged me and said 'bye. With my suitcase in one hand and my trophy in the other, I boarded my Greyhound back to Owensboro.

The bus was crowded. I took a seat by a sweet-looking elderly lady. When I sat down, I noticed she was staring at my trophy.

"My first one," I said, sounding all full of myself, I'm sure.

She smiled and then quickly turned more serious. What's she thinking? I wondered.

I didn't have to wonder long.

She said something I have never forgotten in all the years since then. "Son," she told me, "rejoice in the moment. Enjoy your victory." She then grabbed my hand and looked straight into my eyes and said, "Don't take what you've accomplished for granted. Ever."

I guess she could tell by the way I said "my first one" that I thought there would be many, many more. She wanted me to appreciate any and all of my victories, however few or many that turned out to be.

Because of the life lesson that sweet lady taught me that night, I did just that. I hugged each trophy and enjoyed each win like there wouldn't be another. Fortunately, thanks to his Bobby and his fast go-kart, I was hugging about one a week that summer.

When that summer began, I was definitely a momma's boy because of all the time I spent with her. But some things were beginning to happen to me. I was doing manly stuff, growing closer to my brother and my father. I was already close to my sisters because they had just about raised me. Now, Bobby was making time for me too. That helped me grow up a lot.

CHAPTER 5

CAR READY

Racing with Bobby made that summer the best ever. But success had me wanting to take on new challenges. What I really wanted was my own go-kart.

There was a lot of racing around Kentucky and Indiana nearer to Owensboro. So why was I on a bus every weekend to Tennessee when there was all this racing around home? I loved racing with brother Bobby, but if I had my own kart, I'd be able to drive more tracks against better competition. I have to admit I was beginning to wonder how much good beating those same three kids in Tennessee was doing me.

That fall, I met a family in town who traveled all over the area to race go-karts. The Greens lived down the road from us, and I began to go to their house to watch them work on their go-karts. The dad, the grandpa, and all three kids were in the garage working together. I really thought that was cool. I became good friends with Jeff, the youngest of the three boys. One day Jeff said if I got a go-kart, they would help me work on it and maybe even haul it around for me. Now if I just had a kart! To get a kart, what I needed was a sponsor, someone to pay for my go-kart, my parts, and my pieces. You know, all the stuff I'd asked Darrell to do.

A sponsor in those days was someone who had money and liked racing. I suppose it's not too different today. Sponsors were just as hard to find then as they are now. But I got lucky. A businessman in Owensboro who had helped Darrell back when he was racing locally said he might just help me. Jeff knew a guy, Tommy Tichenor, who was wanting to sell his go-kart and extra parts for $600, and the businessman agreed to cover it. Just like that, I was rolling.

Bobby got me started, and now people who had helped Darrell get going sixteen years earlier were helping me too. Bobby's help was direct and personal. Darrell was helping indirectly, too, by winning races all over the place and making my last name significant in racing circles. I appreciated both their contributions. I remembered something I'd heard my dad, the networker, say over and over again: "It ain't what you know, it's who you know." As I was discovering, that certainly applied to building a racing career.

Once I got my kart and we got it all set up, it was time to go racing. The first place we headed was Olney, Illinois. And man, did things look different in Olney. First of all, the track was about five times bigger than the one I'd been racing on in Smyrna, and there were way more turns. Go-karts were all over the place. When I raced at Smyrna, it was pretty much just racers from that area.

The Olney race was hosted by the Southern Indiana Racing Association. They put on races all over the Midwest, so some of the racers came from a long way away to compete. Instead of the three kids in Smyrna I'd been going against, it looked like at least twenty people would be in my race that day.

Not just a bunch of kids either. Some of the dudes in my race had mustaches!

I was probably the least experienced, and my kart was good but just comparable to the others'. Much to everyone's surprise, including mine, I made a late-race pass on a guy named Greg Bennett and drove off for the win. How did that just happen? I wondered. This was all new to me. Big track and tough competition—and there I stood holding the trophy!

This trophy was about three feet tall. In Victory Lane, I was smiling, proud of what I'd accomplished. But at the same time I was missing Bobby. He had been there for all my races. I loved seeing how proud my brother was of me after the races. He was down in Tennessee racing himself, so he couldn't be there.

The go-kart races were a family thing—moms and dads, brothers and sisters and cousins, all pitching in and working together. Not for me. No Bobby. No Darrell. No Mom and Dad.

Riding home, it was just me and my buddy Kerry, who was kind of becoming my mechanic. Jeff rode home with his family. Despite holding the trophy and having an amazing win under my belt, I was still a little sad on my way back to Kentucky that night. None of my relatives had been there to share my win with me. At least Kerry didn't smoke.

After a couple of very successful years of karting, I was itching to move up. I wanted to race stock cars. Kerry had been building a race car in his garage for a couple of years. It was a Mercury Capri that he planned to race in the mini-modified division at our local track. Kerry was very smart and could make anything. He had pretty much built the whole car—engine and all—by himself. He wanted to be a race-car driver too. When Kerry got his car all together, he took it out to the Kentucky Motor Speedway, the track where all aspiring race-car drivers in Owensboro went to see if they had what it took. He did okay on the track but not great. It was very obvious to me who should be driving Kerry's car. Me! Now I just needed to convince Kerry. My plan was simple: Kerry lets me test the car. If I go faster than Kerry does, I drive.

That made sense, right?

It took a lot of persuading, but Kerry agreed to give me a shot. Not only did I go faster than Kerry when it was my turn, I went faster than everyone else too. I was making laps that day, my first time ever in a race car, faster than the track record. In a noble move, Kerry conceded. "The ride is yours," he said.

His nobility came with one minor condition. I had to buy the tires and help Kerry pay the parts bill he had accumulated while building the car. We got all of our parts from NAPA, by the way.

There I was, back to needing a sponsor again.

I was just a teenager, but I was beginning to get a real appreciation for these sponsor people. The combination of me being able to drive and someone else being able to pay for it was the reason I got to race. That appreciation has never gone away. See NAPA reference above.

But for some reason, the man who sponsored my go-kart didn't think I was ready for stock cars yet. Clearly, he was wrong. But when he pulled his support, it was just me and Kerry.

I had a pretty good job for an eighteen-year-old. My dad had put me to work at Pepsi. I was making $4.35 an hour, and that was a lot. Before I got hired at Pepsi, I had worked at Wendy's for a week. And Wendy's only paid $2.65 an hour, minimum wage, and I did not like working there. One night I cut my finger on a tomato slicer and that was it. I never went back. Working at Wendy's was way too dangerous for me.

Despite the premium wages I was bagging at Pepsi, I didn't have the money to buy tires and pay parts bills. Fortunately for me, however, all the winning I'd done in go-karts had finally gotten my dad's attention. Dad asked his bosses at Pepsi in Evansville if I could paint my car like Darrell's Cup car that year. Darrell was sponsored by Pepsi's Mountain Dew brand. They agreed and bought me a set of brand-new Goodyear tires. I still hadn't come up with enough money to pay the bill at NAPA, but the tires secured me the ride.

But there I was: Opening day, a beautiful Sunday afternoon in Owensboro, Kentucky, at the Kentucky Motor Speedway. I'm telling you, I was looking good, and I was feeling good too. My car was painted just like my big brother's. And unlike when I started in go-karts, my family was there to watch. Mom, Dad, Bobby, my sisters—they were all there to cheer me on.

All the same cars that were there the day I tested were in the pit area. I was feeling very confident. I was faster than any of them at the test, and I'd be faster than all of them again, I was sure.

But then, out of the corner of my eye, I saw a big truck pull into the pits. "Who's that?" I wondered aloud. "That's a fancy rig."

We had a sharp race car. The #11 Mountain Dew Mercury Capri looked awesome. But we hauled our car to the track behind Kerry's old truck. We looked like farmers. Not these cats. Their truck was painted up like their race car. Where were these guys from? Tennessee plates, I noticed. And wow! Their crew guys, they had matching uniforms! As I got a better look at the side of the truck, I could see written in big letters: Driver: NEWT MOORE IV. "Aw, shoot!" I thought to myself. "I'll bet he's really fast."

Suddenly, my confidence was shrinking. As well it should have been. That Newt sucker could move!

In qualifying, Newt won the pole with a new track record. I was second. He won both the preliminary events. Again, I was second. I was already starting to dislike this Newt Moore IV person, and I didn't even know him. Now it was time for the main event. As I buckled in, I tried to figure out how I was going to beat this Nashville cat and his uniform-wearing crew.

The main event was a twenty-five-lapper. When the green flag waved, Newt and I quickly grabbed the top two spots—me leading and Newt right on my bumper. With about five to go, Newt made his move and passed me, just like he had done in the two prelims. But this time, when he drove by, his car slipped, and he drifted up the bank. The door was open for me to slide to the inside and retake the lead. I made the cross-over move perfectly. I'd seen Darrell make that same move. I just reacted. And it worked. I took the lead and held off Newt Moore IV for the win. My first big win on my first night out. And I had to conquer a giant to do it. It was a true David-versus-Goliath story, and Mikey won.

When I grabbed the checkered flag, it felt so perfect. What a race! What a win!

Dad came out on the track to congratulate me. When I pulled into the pit after my victory lap, my whole family was there, as was my crew of three—Kerry, Barry, and Barry—all dressed in different shirts.

What a moment that was!

That turned out to be a big summer for me. I graduated from Apollo High School, barely. I won the track championship at the Speedway by a lot. I was eighteen years old, and I asked myself: "What am I doing still living at home?" With all I had going on, what I needed was a place of my own. My buddy Scott Mercer agreed with me. He thought it was time to get out on his own too.

I knew he'd be the perfect roommate. If you made a list of the most responsible eighteen-year-olds in Owensboro, Kentucky, in 1981, neither of our names would have made it. There might have been a Mike or a Scott on there, but it wouldn't have been either of us.

Scott came from a family of farmers. They raised tobacco, beans, and corn. His job was to work in the fields. His parents provided well for Scott. He had a nice car and always had plenty of spending money. The family lived in a big house out in the country. Heck, they even had their own gas pump. Don't tell anyone, but sometimes late at night, Scott would let me slip in there and fill up with gas. The gas was made for the farm equipment. But it worked fine in our cars. Scott had a hot-rod Oldsmobile. I was driving around in my mom's 1972 four-door Ford Gran Torino, affectionately known to all my friends as "Margaret's car."

Don't laugh at the car. Mom's Ford had two very long bench seats and a customized Kraco car stereo I installed myself with a little bit of help from my brother-in-law Dave. I only needed his help when I got done and turned it on and nothing happened. He had to uncross a couple of wires for me. When my friends and I wanted to take chicks to the drive-in movies, everybody wanted to be in Margaret's car.

Scott and I took time off from our day jobs. We looked around and found a two-bedroom, two-bath villa. Rent was three hundred bucks a month. It was an affordable villa. We agreed Scott would pay a little bit more and take the big bedroom with its own bath. That made sense to me. He could afford to pay more. Now it was just a matter of us breaking the news to our parents. I was pretty sure Mom and Dad would be okay with me moving out. All my brothers and sisters had left home early. What I was uncertain about was whether they'd be okay with me taking Mom's car. I couldn't afford a car *and* an apartment. The keys to Margaret's car were key to the move.

Then I thought: "Who am I kiddin'? I'm sure they want me to move. Taking the old Ford with me won't matter." And I was right.

I walked into the house and told Mom and Dad: "Me and Mercer got an apartment. I'm moving out."

Dad didn't miss a beat. "Good," he said. "Take that damn waterbed with you." I'm surprised he didn't also throw a garden hose at me.

I knew he never liked that waterbed.

I packed my stuff, and I was getting ready to walk out the door. "Well, I'm leaving," I said.

"All right," my dad said, barely looking up from his chair. "You'll be back."

"No, I won't. I'm movin'."

"Okay, we'll see ya."

"Well, 'bye then."

I wasn't looking for any tears. But I thought at least somebody would get up and give me a hug.

I went straight to Mercer's house to help him get his stuff together. The scene was very different there. His mom was sitting on the couch sobbing. His dad had a concerned look on his face. "You're too young," his mom wailed. "It's too soon. You can't move out. You don't know what you're doin'. Don't go." It was like he was moving to California to join a cult. Man, his parents didn't want to let go.

You know that saying "If you love somebody, you gotta let 'em go"? I knew my parents really loved me. And I wanted to show them how much I appreciated that. So when I moved out, I moved on, and I never moved back.

PART 2:
DRIVING

CHAPTER 6

FINDING RIDES

Back in the day, if you dreamed of racing with the big boys, you had to get there one step at a time.

There was a set pattern. You got your start on local tracks running modifieds or late-models or whatever you could get behind the wheel of. If you won some races, then you'd move up to Dash Series if you could. This was entry-level NASCAR. These cars were four-cylinder subcompacts, but they were real race cars.

The Dash cars would compete on tracks like Daytona and Darlington and Atlanta and North Wilkesboro. You got to race on the same tracks on the same weekends the Cup stars did. You did well there, people would notice.

After Dash, the next logical thing to do would be to move up to the NASCAR Busch Series. At every step, the competition got tougher and tougher. The cars got faster and faster. The driving took more skill. And if you were successful in the Busch Series, you just might have what it took to make it into Winston Cup, the pinnacle of NASCAR racing. That was the perfect road map to racing stardom.

But my opportunity didn't come that way.

My early years of racing couldn't have gone any better. All I did was win. In 1981, I won my first race at my local track. I went on to win the track championship there. In the '81 season, it didn't matter what the challenge was, I met it. Whether I was racing as a rookie making my first start or racing for a championship, I won. I was a winner. The sky's the limit, I thought. I got this. I'll be just like my brother. He was winning. He won the '81 NASCAR Cup Series championship. He repeated it in '82. I was racing locally and beginning to take my car to other tracks.

In 1982, I ran a couple of races in the Dash Series. I did well and got a ride in 1983 with one of the top teams in Dash—Richard Mash Racing. The winning continued. I won a record number of pole positions in '83. I won six races that year. I was the most popular driver in the series. I got my first NASCAR championship trophy, the first of many, I was sure.

There I went again!

That kinda sounds like the little boy who got on the bus that day back in Kentucky, don't you think? All full of himself about what he had accomplished. It was important for me to remember the lesson that little old lady had taught me—not to take winning, or these trophies, for granted. Be thankful, always. But things were really going well with my career. That one year, 1983, had taken me from the local track in Kentucky to winning in small cars on the big tracks of NASCAR. Now I just needed to figure out what my next step would be.

After the 1983 season, I moved to Louisville to work at Komfort Koach. They had become my sponsor during the 1983 championship season. Komfort Koach was a luxury custom-van conversion company. The president was Bill Borden. Bill loved NASCAR and provided NASCAR officials and some drivers with their own vans in exchange for advertising and endorsements. Darrell had a Komfort Koach van. So did Richard Petty. I moved to Louisville to work for Bill because I needed to be able to travel more if I was going to pursue my racing dreams.

Living in Owensboro, working for Dad at Pepsi, was getting to be too difficult. With all the time I was gone, my paycheck wasn't enough to keep gas in my car. All I was paying for were my travel expenses, and I couldn't even do that anymore. Bill said I could live with his family and work at the van factory during the week. And I could travel as I needed. Bill would still pay me even when I was off racing. That sounded like a much better deal to me than working at the Pepsi plant. Even when I wasn't there, I'd get paid. I liked that. But working for Komfort Koach in Louisville was just a stepping-stone for me to get to North Carolina. That's where I really had to be. You couldn't build a NASCAR career living in Kentucky, working on vans. That's not where the action was. That was like being a country singer and not living in Nashville.

Fortunately, Bill's connection to the NASCAR world wasn't just through his sponsorships. He had become friends with lots of NASCAR people as well. After I'd been with the Bordens for six months or so, Bill, knowing I wanted to be down south, had worked it out for me to move down there. He actually pawned me off on Kyle Petty, a racer and real prince of a guy. Actually, a NASCAR prince. His dad was Richard Petty, the King.

I went to live with Kyle and his wife, Pattie, and their children, Adam, Austin, and Montgomery Lee, and work at Petty Enterprises. Finally my job was to work on race cars, not flip burgers, deliver soft drinks, or fix some dumb van. I had always worked on my own race cars. But now I was working on Kyle's cars, the cars that he raced in NASCAR. And I was getting paid. All I had to do for rent at Kyle's house was keep my room clean and occasionally watch the kids.

The oldest of the three, Adam, he was a real pistol. He used to tell me he was going to be a race-car driver just like his daddy and his grandpa. The family lived on a lake way out in the country, and sometimes I'd let Adam sit in my lap and drive when it was just me and him. He got a real kick out of that.

Living with Kyle was going really well for a few months. Then came the infamous tennis-shoe incident. My shoes stunk. They were old. Most all of my stuff was old, but it was all I had. I woke up one morning and my shoes were missing. I asked Kyle if he'd seen them.

"Yeah, I saw 'em," he said. "I'd guess they're floating down by the dam about now."

"Why would they be at the dam?" I asked.

"Because," he said, "you left them lying in the middle of the living room floor, and they stunk. So I threw 'em in the lake."

This wasn't good, I sensed. I was guessing if my shoes got thrown out the back door, it wouldn't be long before my ass got thrown out the front.

So on the way to work that day, I began thinking about what I was going to do next. I had a long time to ponder that. It was about an hour's drive to work from Kyle's house.

"I have a job now," I thought. "Maybe I'll just get an apartment or something."

But before I left work that same day, Lynda Petty, Kyle's mom, approached me and asked if I wanted to move in with her and the King.

"It's a long drive out to Kyle's," she said. "And we live right around the corner from the shop."

"I'd love to," I said. "Thank you very much. I'll be there tonight."

Then I thought, "Wow! Kyle just kicked me out of his house. I've never seen it done quite so nicely."

Later that night I showed up at Lynda and Richard Petty's house in Randleman, North Carolina. It looked a little dark, but I nervously rang the doorbell. Richard opened the door. I think it was the first time I'd ever seen him without his hat and sunglasses.

"Hey, buddy," he said in his thick Carolina accent. "I hear you're coming to live with us. Where's all your stuff?"

"It's just me and my suitcase," I said. "This is about all I got. I used to have another pair of shoes, but your son threw 'em in the lake."

Living with Richard was cool. He was a night owl. We used to sit on the couch well past midnight some nights, eating popcorn and talking about racing. A pattern was developing here, I suppose. Anytime I could sit around and talk about something, that something was racing. It started with my dad at McDonald's in Kentucky. Same thing when I got in the car and drove down the road with my brother Bobby. And now I was sitting on the couch with Richard Petty, talking racing to him. I had a one-track mind.

At this point in my life, 1985, there was one person I hadn't had the opportunity to talk racing with. That was Darrell. We just couldn't find time to do something like that.

I loved hanging out with the King. We were friends. One night he asked me about my racing plans.

"I got a great plan," I told him. "So far, I've done everything by the book."

I explained I'd won in go-karts. Then I'd won in stock cars at my local track. Then the NASCAR Dash Series championship. "Now I gotta get to Busch," I told him.

Richard didn't answer me directly. He just asked a question. "What's your goal?" he wanted to know.

I told him straight out. "My goal," I said, "is to make it to the Winston Cup Series and win races just like you."

"If that's what you want to do," he said, "then that's what you should do now. You need to go race Cup right now. You don't need to be messin' around with those Busch cars. You just need to get a Cup ride.

"What are you, twenty-one, twenty-two years old?" Richard asked. "You need to start getting experience in the cars you want to end up in. You will just be wasting your time in a Busch car."

Hmm, I thought. Interesting. That's an idea I'd never heard or thought of.

"All right," I said. "Sounds good to me, Rich. I'm just wondering though. How exactly am I gonna do that? Are you asking me to drive for Petty Enterprises?"

I was joking. The King looked at me like I was kinda stupid. "Just kidding," I said.

Back then, established teams didn't hire kids like they do now. You had to be experienced to get a Cup ride. And in order to get that experience, you had to race Busch, I thought.

Not according to Richard. "Go get a Cup ride," he said. "Figure it out."

And that was indeed what I was going to do. This was Richard Petty giving me career direction. I had to figure this out.

Getting a Cup ride was now my focus. At work that day I asked around the shop to see if any of the guys had any ideas. No one really came up with anything. So the following night the scene was the same. Late-night popcorn on the couch with the King.

I told Richard I'd asked around and hadn't come up with any ideas. I didn't want to be aggravating. But I was hoping he had some ideas for me.

"Can you give me a little more direction here?" I asked him.

The King thought for a minute and then said: "Maybe you should go see Humpy Wheeler at Charlotte Motor Speedway. The World 600 is coming up over there in a few weeks. Ask him if he'll help you get started."

I'd heard of Humpy Wheeler before. He was a track promoter extraordinaire. He liked to be an innovator. The track promoter's ultimate responsibility was to have fans in the stands. And Humpy wasn't so particular how he got them there, just as long as they came. For example, his pre-race shows were legendary. He had motorcyclists jumping school buses, junk cars catching on fire—you name it, he did it. One of his pre-race stunts involved fireworks. A spark hit the owner of the track,

Bruton Smith, and set his hair on fire. I think Bruton might have been wearing too much hair spray.

Humpy also cared about the sport. He made sure if there was young talent who needed a little help to get started, to provide that help. I know he helped Dale Earnhardt get his start. Tim Richmond too.

Go see Humpy. That's what I was gonna do.

So I was off to see a man named Humpy. I wondered if I'd be able to work my way through the layers of people surrounding him. Would this Humpy man be willing to help me? Would he catch me on fire?

As I drove toward the Charlotte Motor Speedway, I considered my options. I wondered how I should open the conversation with Humpy. Should I say, "Hello, I'm Michael Waltrip, Darrell's little brother"? Or should I say, "Humpy, Michael Waltrip here, 1983 NASCAR Dash Series champion."

I liked the way that one sounded. And I knew I had in my pocket the fact that Richard Petty had sent me. I could use that if I needed it.

When I got there, I decided to go with "Michael Waltrip, Darrell's little brother." I needed to use all the star power I could muster. And it worked. His secretary told Humpy I was there and he came right out.

"Hello there, young man," Humpy said, reaching his hand.

Back then, I wasn't quite the sophisticated, debonair gentleman that I am today. So I suppose when I reached out to shake Humpy's hand, I must have kind of looked away. I was a bit nervous just being there. That nervousness got a lot worse during this handshake.

Humpy grabbed my hand and wouldn't let go. He squeezed it tighter and tighter. Humpy is quite athletic. He was a Golden Gloves boxer when he was growing up. His grip got my attention for sure, and he knew it.

"Son," he said, "look people in the eye when you shake hands." He was serious.

"Yes, sir," I said.

To this day, that is something I've never forgotten. Every time I shake someone's hand, I think of ol' Humpy. Once we got that behind us, I explained to him why I was there. I wanted to race the World 600. "Richard Petty suggested I come see you," I said.

Humpy and I had a great conversation, and he directed me to go see a man named Dick Bahre. Like me, Dick had moved South. He came from Maine to pursue his dream of owning a NASCAR team. Dick had run a few races, so he had the cars and engines—just about everything you needed to race with. Just about everything. The one thing he was missing? Money.

That seemed to be the theme here. Racing took money. And it seemed all the racers I met didn't have any.

But all the same, I gave Dick Bahre a call. I told him that Humpy Wheeler had suggested I come and see him and figure out if there was some way I could drive his car at Charlotte that month.

I didn't know what to expect from Dick. I'd never been to New England. But the man I met sure didn't fit the stereotype I had in my mind. I was thinking about Nantucket and clamming and maybe sailing in khaki pants and one of those sweaters that doesn't have any sleeves. Maybe this guy wasn't Dick? But he had to be. He was the only one there, and his name was on his work shirt. On one pocket, it said: "Dick." On the other it said: "Dick Bahre Racing." So I put two and two together. Dick was working on a rear-end housing for one of his race cars. He had welded it up and was grinding the weld down with the biggest grinder I had ever seen. It looked like something you'd be grinding on a tank with, not on any race car I'd ever seen.

Dick was a tall, lanky man, but with smoke rolling off the cigar in his mouth and sparks flying off the grinder, he looked like a character from one of the *Terminator* movies. I just stood there and waited for him to look up.

When he finally noticed me, he shut the grinder down and turned his attention my way. "How ya doin', there?" Dick asked. His sweet, friendly demeanor didn't match the tough guy I was looking at. To this day, I've never met a nicer, kinder, gentler man.

There were literally dozens of guys with shops and a race car I could have walked in on in the Charlotte area who would have said, "Yeah, you bring me a little bit of money and you can drive my car"—then taken the money and gone on to the next naïve, unsuspecting dreamer. Dick was exactly the opposite of that.

Not only did he let me drive his car and tell me whatever help I could get was fine, he continued to invest in me, running race after race with way less sponsorship money than it cost to race.

"Come up with whatever you can," he told me that first day. "We'll go over to Charlotte and give it a try."

Seriously? I thought. Sounds like I got the ride. Does that mean I'm a Cup driver now?

He didn't even ask to see my résumé. Good thing, because I didn't have one. My résumé, if I'd had one, would have consisted of me winning a Dash Series championship in little cars that were the polar opposite of a Cup car.

I called Humpy and told him I had the ride for Charlotte. I asked him if he could help Dick out. Humpy agreed to help with the tire bill. And just like that, I became a Cup driver and a darn good hand-shaker—all in the same day.

CHAPTER 7

CUP DEBUT

Richard Petty sent me to Humpy Wheeler, who sent me to Dick Bahre. Within a few days of moving in with Richard, I had a ride in the World 600.

If it weren't for the King, I might still be sitting around trying to follow my lame plan. Instead, I was going to be driving Dick Bahre's 1985 Chevrolet Monte Carlo with #23 on the side. It was the Memorial Day weekend NASCAR race at the Charlotte Motor Speedway.

My experience was admittedly minimal—okay, almost none—in a car like this one. This baby was big. It had a 358-cubic-inch V8 engine in it. It had maybe double the horsepower of anything I had ever driven anywhere.

The mini-modifieds I'd raced back in Kentucky? They had little four-bangers in them. The Dash Series cars? Same thing. Small motor, no power. This was going to be a major step up for me. I'd be sitting in one of the most powerful race cars in the world, a NASCAR Winston Cup stock car. This was a man's machine, and it felt like one too. I'm six-foot-five. Squeezing into those mini-modifieds and Dash cars was a pain in the neck. Literally. I had to tilt my head to the side to see through the windshield. But in that Cup car, I had plenty of room. Heck, Wilt Chamberlain would have had plenty of room.

And oh, by the way, when I was sitting in that baby with all that room, looking out that windshield so clearly—I was going to be looking at Richard Petty, David Pearson, and Darrell Waltrip all racing on the same track with me. That was a little hard to comprehend. Barely a decade earlier, I was in the backseat of Mom and Dad's Chevy heading south to watch these guys, dreaming of being one of them one day. That day was here. I was going to be racing with the greats in the World 600.

If I could accomplish one thing.

It was kind of a big thing.

I needed to qualify for the race.

Practice was on Wednesday. To say I was intimidated would be like saying the *Titanic* sprung a small leak. Think pulling onto the track that first time ever in Bobby's go-kart was scary? This was way worse. No one was watching then.

If I'd screwed up on Bobby's go-kart, Bobby would have been mad. If I went out now and messed up and I took Richard Petty or Darrell Waltrip with me? The whole NASCAR world would be mad.

But just like that day in Smyrna, Tennessee, when I hit the track, I wasn't nervous anymore. I was just focused. When I got on the back straightaway and put my right foot on the floorboard, the action picked up considerably. Suddenly I felt like I was in a wrestling match with some-body way bigger than me—maybe a couple of people. I felt like I'd driven the cars I'd raced prior to this one. But this car, with all its power and all its girth—mostly, I was along for the ride. That sucker had a mind of its own. As I wrestled that car around the track, it didn't take but a lap or two for me to realize how much I had to learn.

I really felt like a rookie. I hadn't experienced anything like this. By the time most guys make their Cup debut, they've been racing big, power-ful cars like this one on dirt tracks and short tracks all over the South. I was mad at that stupid Dash car now. I felt like such a wimp. That wasn't racing. Those cars were easy to drive. I thought I was somebody, winning those races and that championship. But that hadn't done any-thing to prepare me for the path the King had put me on.

Heck, Dale Earnhardt won a race in his rookie year. I'd be lucky to qualify.

So I had to learn it quickly. Qualifying was just a couple of hours away. I thought I was a pretty good driver, but I was beginning to rethink that. I was having a hard time driving this car. It was driving me—crazy.

By the time practice had ended, my crew told me I'd run some pretty good lap times. With my lack of experience and trying to understand this car, I was having trouble putting consistent laps together. But when I did it right, I was pretty fast. First-round qualifying for the 600 would lock in the first fifteen positions. The 600 was the only race during the season where qualifying consisted of four laps. They took all four of your laps and averaged them together. Whoever had the fastest four-lap average won the pole.

Luckily, there was a second round of qualifying. Because round one didn't go so well for me.

The inconsistency I'd struggled with in practice was the issue again. My four-lap average wasn't good because my second two laps were really slow.

In second-round qualifying the next day, it was just straight up your fastest lap—one lap to get in the race. I felt confident about being able to run one lap fast enough to make the World 600 field. And I did. My speed locked me into twenty-fourth position. Heck, I even beat Richard Petty in my first Cup attempt!

Richard came by and told me, "You done good there"—or something like that. Whatever it was, it made me smile. Then he said: "Make sure you get out of my way when they throw the green flag Sunday."

He walked off. I wondered if he was kidding or he was serious.

Was he being Richard Petty, my landlord? Telling me if I liked where I lived, I'd get out of his way? Or was he being Richard Petty, the racer, who didn't want this rookie holding him up?

Whichever way it was, I was going to get out of the King's way. He was the one who came up with this whole idea. I couldn't believe that it was just a couple of weeks earlier I was lying on his couch with no idea what was coming next.

Now the King had just congratulated me for, of all things, out-qualifying him. But he also left me with a little dose of reality, reminding me to get the hell out of his way.

That's how things were going for me, steady progress at breakneck speed. And here I was, qualified for my first NASCAR Winston Cup race.

But for the very first time, I wasn't thinking about winning. This Cup car had made me second-guess what I'd been doing career-wise up to this point.

It was a different breed, this hotrod. I wasn't going to win at Charlotte. But hopefully I'd catch on quick so I could continue my winning ways.

I was trying to build myself back up. I must be pretty good, I thought. This is the first time I tried to qualify, and I did it.

But I didn't like the way that big ol' car felt at all. I wished I'd learned to drive one of these when nobody was looking—instead of right on NASCAR's center stage. A little late to be worrying about that now.

Another thing that had never dawned on me: They didn't call this race the World 600 just because they thought it sounded catchy. That 600 meant something—600 miles, my first race in NASCAR and the longest race of the year.

That's about how far it was from Owensboro to Daytona. That was a scary thought. And this time, I wouldn't be able to listen to Roy Clark.

Just four years earlier, I had run my first stock-car race, that twenty-five-lapper on a quarter-mile track. You do the math. That's Aaron's slogan: "Nobody beats Aaron's." Aw, man, there I go again. My first race was all of about six miles long. The Dash Series races were as long as a hundred and fifty miles. And I thought those were marathons. But we're talking about six hundred miles on a hot afternoon in May with this beast of a race car while sharing the track with NASCAR's greatest.

What the heck was I doing here?

I knew I had to focus on my goals, which were going to be very different this time.

First goal: Stay out of the way.

Second goal: Finish the race.

I knew I had to stay out of Richard Petty's way. He'd already told me so. And Kyle Petty's. He'd been my landlord too. I also needed to give him extra room. And my brother DW, of course. We hadn't really talked, but I figured I'd better give him some space. And Bill Elliott would be racing for a million dollars that day, a bonus offered by series sponsor Winston for winning three of the four biggest races of the year. Bill had already won two of them. If he won today, he'd have one million dollars. What if I screwed that up?

So as the race started I had these four guys on my brain. And that was messing with me. It seemed like about every lap, one of them was either passing me or catching me. I was driving looking in the mirror. That isn't any way to go about racing a car. I needed to be looking ahead to learn, not looking back.

My speed was suffering, too. I couldn't even keep up with the guys I was used to seeing run last. That was getting frustrating. Everyone was passing me.

But I stayed reasonably focused and remembered my goals. Stay out of the way and finish the race. So I pushed on, every lap trying to learn more about this car and how to drive it. As those laps ticked by, I actually started getting better. I started to improve. Finally, I was beginning to keep up with some of those guys. I actually almost passed one of them.

Goal one was being accomplished. I was staying out of the way. In addition to that, I was learning, and I was starting to like what was going on. But just then, about four hundred and fifty miles in, my transmission went—and with it went goal number two.

My day had its share of frustration in the World 600. But all things considered, I was happy with what I'd achieved. I wound up being scored twenty-eighth in the finishing order. I'd run my first Cup race. And I hadn't made anyone mad.

And guess who won that day?

Ol' DW.

Darrell, our mom and dad, and Darrell's team were celebrating in Victory Lane just a couple of hundred yards from where my team and I were staring at a broken transmission. I knew DW was smelling and tasting NASCAR's finest champagne. Brut, I suspect. But all I could smell was burnt transmission fluid. Sunoco, I suspect.

We were literally only a couple hundred yards apart. But the distance between Margaret and Leroy's two Cup drivers might as well have been a million miles. There's a lot of difference between a Cup driver and a Cup winner. I was just beginning my journey.

The first step was recapping with my team the 600 week in Charlotte. Everybody involved agreed: My first Cup start was a success. I did a good job out there, making the race and running most of it. I logged laps, and I logged a lot of experience. More important, I earned the respect of some of my heroes on the track. But the main guy I needed to impress was my car owner, Dick Bahre. He was paying the bills, all of them except for the help Humpy gave us. If Dick was happy, maybe we could do this again. And Dick was happy.

I remember him chewing on cigar in his trademark cowboy boots and work shirt, smiling, and saying: "We turned some heads out there today. Let's do that again."

And that's exactly what we did. We ran four more races in 1985. We performed a little bit better each week.

My best finish came at Michigan, where I ended up eighteenth. Dick and I were able to secure a bit of sponsorship for the 1986 season, and we ran the whole year. That was the first of twenty-four straight years of me racing in the NASCAR Cup Series full-time.

Thanks to what I'd learned from my dad, I was able to network my way right into Cup. From Bill Borden to Kyle to Richard to Humpy to Dick. That was the path to my first Cup race.

Even today, twenty-five years later, all those people hold special places in my heart.

CHAPTER 8

MEETING DALE

We were in Darlington, South Carolina, in 1986. The Darlington Raceway was tough. This track even had nicknames: "Too Tough to Tame" and the "Lady in Black."

Late in the going, Dale Earnhardt, the Man in Black, was leading the Southern 500. Those two made a pretty good pair. If anyone could tame her, it would have been Dale. I was having a pretty good run for a rookie that day, as long as you didn't compare my rookie season to Dale's.

I was running up in the top ten with just twenty or thirty laps to go in the 367-lap, 500-mile race. It was hot, I was tired, the end was near, and I was glad. I came off turn two, swung out to the wall, and made my way down the backstretch for what seemed like about the thousandth time.

Suddenly, out of nowhere, Dale was right beside me, looking over and pointing his finger at me. Back then you could totally see into another guy's car, and I could see Dale wasn't happy. I had cut him off coming out of turn two. Dale had cut me a break and didn't wipe me out. He could probably tell by the sloppy way I was driving that I wasn't exactly as focused in the final laps as I should have been.

I don't know if you've ever been to Darlington in September. But if you have, you know it gets a little toasty there. I'd had about all the racing I wanted for the day. I didn't know Dale that well yet. But I knew the Intimidator, the driver who had just pointed his finger at me and driven off toward turn three.

I could imagine him saying: "You don't know how lucky you are, boy. I coulda just busted your butt. Keep your shit together. These races are five hundred miles. This ain't one of those sissy-ass Dash races. This is the big time."

I met Dale Earnhardt when I first showed up in 1983. By then, Dale was already a giant personality and a NASCAR champion. In the racing world, most everybody lived in awe of Dale, including me. We definitely didn't become instant friends or anything. Like a lot of people, he probably only knew who I was because of Darrell. Dale and Darrell didn't like each other too much. That was obvious. But I figured Dale knew Darrell hadn't exactly gone out of his way to help me get started, yet somehow there I was, making my way through the lower divisions of NASCAR. He probably appreciated that.

Dale grew up in the North Carolina town of Kannapolis. Racing was in his blood. His dad, Ralph Earnhardt, was one of the best short-track drivers around, although he never made it in racing's big time. Dale's father did what he could to discourage his son's racing dreams, just as mine had. But Mr. Earnhardt's efforts failed as miserably as Mr. Waltrip's had. Maybe more so. Ralph worried that if Dale didn't complete his education he'd be stuck in one of the cotton mills around Kannapolis. But Dale dropped out of school when he was sixteen to pursue racing, disappointing his dad badly.

Dale told me his dad was tough on him. He wasn't always patient or supportive. Ralph died of a heart attack in 1973, when Dale was twenty-two. The fact that he had dropped out of high school and let his dad down haunted Dale. I think it pushed him to prove himself early, which he got busy doing at the local short tracks.

And Ralph's boy, he could drive! Whether on dirt or asphalt, he would win.

In his rookie NASCAR season of 1979, Dale won the race at Bristol, captured four poles, had eleven top-five finishes and seventeen in the top ten. He finished seventh in points despite missing four races because of a broken collarbone.

When I said not to compare my rookie season to Dale's, these numbers are the reason why. My stat columns were full of zeroes. No wins. No poles. No top fives. No top tens. In my defense, most rookies' results look more like mine than Dale's.

But Dale was special. If he hadn't gotten hurt in his rookie season, he would have been a contender for the championship. He proved that the next year. Right off the bat at Daytona, Dale won the Busch Clash, a special event for all the pole winners from the previous season. Then he took Atlanta, Bristol, Nashville, Martinsville, and Charlotte, winning his first of seven Winston Cup championships. Dale's the only driver ever to follow up Rookie of the Year with the Cup championship.

Although I was around from '83 on and had met Dale's glare eye-to-eye on the track, he and I didn't speak much, if at all, until '86. That was my rookie season in Cup and the year that Dale won his second championship.

The championship banquet in those days was held in the Waldorf-Astoria Hotel's Grand Ballroom in New York City. NASCAR would invite all the drivers in the top twenty in points to join in honoring the championship team. I finished nineteenth in the standings that year and made my first trip to the Big Apple. And what did I do when I got to town? Went straight to my room and got room service. And watched TV. I had a lot to learn about that big city. The next night, Dale and his wife, Teresa, started a tradition that carried on for many years. They held a gathering for some of the race-car drivers and owners and their wives in their suite, the presidential suite. Drinks were served. And it sometimes turned into lots of drinks. There were hors d'oeuvres too. The champion had a lot of responsibilities during that week in New York. We all thought it was very gracious of Dale and Teresa to spend some time with Dale's peers.

And they did it in their hotel room, just like I had the night before. More or less.

Dale was one of those people who seemed at home wherever he was, at the racetrack or in a fancy hotel suite. Just over six feet tall in his trademark Wrangler jeans, gargoyle sunglasses, and cowboy boots, no one pulled off the rough-and-tough look at the track better than Dale did. The first thing you'd notice was those sunglasses and his mustache. He looked like a cowboy who might ride bulls—or fight them. But drop him in New York City in a sport coat and loafers and Dale looked like he could run a corporate board meeting. And he could. He was a very smart man.

At those parties in New York, we had a few pretty interesting conversations. The talk would mostly be racing stories, maybe about what had happened in the course of the season. But my favorite part was when Dale would tell stories about his dirt-track racing days. Wrecking. Winning. And fighting. Then having a few celebratory beers. They'd celebrate the wins. Both wins: the race and the fight. That seemed to be the usual order.

The best way to describe Dale back then was plainspoken. Fifteen years and seven championships later, you'd still describe him the same way. Unadorned. Direct. Frank. Even if you barely knew him, you never had much doubt what Dale Earnhardt thought.

Being with Dale in New York City was an education. Over the years, he taught me where to go for a fine dinner when I finally ventured out of the hotel. We got to hanging out more and more up there. In New York City, he was loose. But not at the track. There, he was the Intimidator. Everyone knew he was that way in the car. He was the same in the pit and around the garage. He always looked pissed off to me. I just steered clear of him. I knew he didn't much like my brother back then, and whatever Darrell had done, I was pretty sure that made me guilty by association. They eventually got over their differences. Darrell even drove a few races for Dale.

Over time, I learned that Dale had a quieter, gentler side. It would come out when we were fishing or spending time together with our families. The people who knew Dale best, a small group I would eventually become part of—we saw a far more complex person than the driver most fans were aware of, a man capable of doing just about anything.

But it was the tough Dale—the death-defying Dale—that most people focused on. That was the one I first got to know.

He picked up his nickname, the Intimidator, in 1987 after a battle with Bill Elliott near the end of the Winston, the high-stakes NASCAR All-Star race. Dale then became the "Man in Black" after GM Goodwrench became his sponsor and the #3 car got a fresh, fittingly intimidating black paint scheme.

The nicknames certainly fit Dale's driving style. He was aggressive, unwavering, and fearless—and maybe a little bit nuts. When he climbed behind the wheel of a race car, Dale didn't think of death. He thought of winning. Looking back at some of Dale's crashes, it's hard to see how he got through as many of them as he did.

Like in July 1996 in Talladega. He and Ernie Irvan got together, setting off a crazy crash that sent Dale head-on into the outside at two hundred miles an hour. Dale's car flipped and slid through traffic across the track. His car was hit in the roof and on the windshield. It didn't look like there was any way anyone could survive that. But Dale climbed right out of the car and waved at the crowd.

In fact, he showed up the next week in Indianapolis and qualified his car. At the first pit stop, a broken collarbone forced him to hand off the wheel to Mike Skinner, one of his Richard Childress Racing teammates. The crash at Talladega didn't bring him to tears. But handing off his car at Indy certainly did. Dale said: "It was the hardest thing I ever had to do."

Then, in true Dale Earnhardt style, the next week he was back in the seat driving his car to the pole at Watkins Glen. That spawned a T-shirt fans bought by the thousands. On the shirt was a picture of Dale's face. The caption read: "It Hurts So Good."

CHAPTER 9

RACING ALONG

Hurts so good. That describes racing a lot of the time. Something good happens, followed by something bad. Your emotions certainly get a workout.

Nineteen eighty-eight was my third full season racing in the NASCAR Winston Cup Series. For the first time in my career, I had a major sponsor, Country Time Lemonade. Things were progressing nicely in Cup with my team. We were running well. I grabbed my first top-five finish that year, a second place at Pocono, Pennsylvania, in July.

But that turned out to be a tough day at the races. My finish was great. But on the first lap of the race, there was a major crash in turn two. NASCAR champion Bobby Allison was critically injured. They had to cut him out of his car and airlift him to the hospital. He had suffered a serious head injury. Bobby wasn't just another racer on the track. He was my friend. Back in 1984, I had practiced and qualified his car for him in Milwaukee.

Bobby raced short tracks all over the country, and sometimes I would go with him to race. So when the checkered flag flew that day in Pocono, I was celebrating my best career finish with my team. But then I found out about my friend and I was worried.

Bobby recovered. But he was never able to race anything again.

Emotional swings in racing are something every driver has to deal with. But it's never easy. That's a lesson I've been forced to learn over and over again.

Our partnership with Country Time was going well. They were using our team to help them sell lots of lemonade. They wanted to expand their partnership with us in NASCAR. The Kroger 200 was a big Busch Series race that was held every August in Indianapolis. Kroger sponsored the race and sold Country Time Lemonade in their stores. So Country Time wanted a car in that race. I was going to get to do something I'd always wanted to do, which was race in the Busch Series.

I'd skipped right over Busch at Richard Petty's suggestion. I went straight from the Dash Series to Winston Cup. I really wanted my shot at running some Busch races. I believed I could beat those guys, and I thought it would be a lot of fun trying. And the truth was that I was missing Victory Lane. After all the winning I'd done getting to the Cup Series, I hadn't won lately.

Racing the Kroger 200 was indeed fun. I didn't win that night, but I qualified fourth and ran competitively in my first Busch Series race. I ended up finishing twelfth.

I wasn't the only Cup driver who thought Busch was fun. Darrell had his own Busch Series team. That was kind of a hobby for him. He owned the car, and he had a sponsor. He did it on the side for fun, the way Dale Earnhardt and Bobby Allison and a lot of other guys back then liked to do. Not surprisingly, Darrell's car had the best equipment money could buy. He had it all. I had always bugged DW about letting me drive his car for him, but he never would let me. My performance in Indy that night, I think, impressed him.

A couple of weeks later, Darrell got a little banged up in a crash at Bristol, Tennessee. He was supposed to drive in the Busch race the next week in Darlington, South Carolina, but his shoulder and ribs were still a little too sore to race, he thought. And guess what? He asked me if I would drive for him.

Well, it's about damn time, I thought. That was a question I'd been waiting to hear forever—or at least since I was about twelve years old.

"Heck, yeah," I answered. "I'd love to. I was beginning to wonder if you were ever gonna ask."

It was a surprise, but it was going to be my second Busch Series start, and I couldn't have been happier. Darrell had already qualified the car. I just had to get in and drive it. And drive it I did, all the way up to a third-place finish behind Harry Gant and Geoff Bodine. And I made that run all the way to the front without any practice. I just jumped in and went.

Darrell had never given me an opportunity to drive his stuff before. But when I got the chance, I stepped up. Went out there and ran third for him, right behind two of NASCAR's biggest stars. Not bad for a last-minute sub. One of the toughest tracks in NASCAR and I hadn't put a scratch on the car.

I was in a perfect position to bargain for more. The bargaining began as soon as I got out of Darrell's car at Darlington that day. "We gotta do this again," I told him. "Let me qualify and practice it next time, and I'll win for you."

"Oh, you think so?" Darrell asked.

"I know so."

"How do you like Dover, Little Bro?" Darrell asked. It was sounding like I was in.

"I love Dover," I said. "It's actually my favorite track." Or at least that's what I said.

Darrell then said, "Dover it is. You can drive for me there."

Every now and then, I get the answer I'm looking for. I went to Dover on a mission to prove to Darrell I was right.

In Darlington, I'd been shocked that morning when he said, "Come drive my car." But I'd been looking forward to this race for two weeks. And when we got to Dover and practice began, I was fast—and very confident I could win.

I guess Darrell was hurting more at Darlington than he let on. He wasn't really involved in race strategy or the talk over the radio between me and the crew. I didn't hear but a few words from him down in South Carolina. But boy, he made up for it at Dover. The first voice I heard over the radio was DW's, and he sounded like an announcer. "Mike, it's DW up top—do you read me?"

"Really well, boss," I replied. "You seem extra loud, for some reason."

I started from the fifth position that day and moved forward from there. I was sitting second just past the three-quarter mark of the race. The caution had come out for an accident, and we were riding around while they cleaned up the track. My brother was on the radio a lot that day. It was getting late in the race, and evidently Darrell was getting nervous.

What I heard over the radio next I'd never heard in a race car before.

Darrell keyed his mic and calmly said: "This is what we got, little brother. There aren't that many laps left. And you're faster than that cat leadin'. You been faster than him all day. We gotta be patient though. We can make a silly mistake this late in the going. We gotta win this race."

He kept going on and on and on.

"You're the wild card," Darrell continued. "These boys ain't never raced with you before. These boys don't know what you got up your sleeve. They're gonna be a little leery of how you're gonna attack 'em."

At this point, I began to think, "Will he ever shut up?"

I felt as if my brother was channeling Vince Lombardi. I half expected him to say, "Winning isn't everything. It's the only thing." Or was that Knute Rockne? I can never remember. I just knew Darrell was getting on my nerves.

After a solid two or three laps of this, he finally took his finger off the talk button. And I quickly pushed mine. What I said was, "What I really need now"—I was trying to be polite—"is for all of you to please be quiet. I know what I have to do, and I'm gonna do it."

And when the green flag flew for the run to the finish, I did it.

I passed Tommy Ellis in the Goo Goo Clusters Buick and won my first NASCAR Busch Series race. My first win, my second ride in Darrell's car in my third Busch Series start. One, two, three—just like that.

Winning that day in my brother's car was so satisfying after how long I'd waited for the opportunity to drive for him. We were standing in Victory Lane, me and Darrell, the guy I'd looked up to since I was a baby. He'd finally given me the chance. And we were holding a trophy together in, of all places, Delaware. We were spraying champagne. Actually, it was Busch beer. But it still felt great. Margaret and Leroy's boys were in Victory Lane together.

We never talked about him paying me. I was pretty sure if I'd have asked him, he would have said: "You should be paying me to drive my car." He was kind of full of himself like that. But I didn't care. I just wanted to race.

The next morning I picked up the paper. It said I'd won something like $10,000. Wow, that's a lot of money! I thought. You see, my car owner in Cup at that time was, let's say, frugal—to put it mildly. I thought, I don't know what he'll give me, but I'll bet it's going to be a lot. A lot more than I usually get.

I was wrong.

Darrell mailed me a check for $1,000. And I thought *my* Cup car owner was tight!

"Ten percent, Darrell?" I said to myself.

One day I was joking around with Darrell and his crew guys. I told them he'd sent me a check for ten percent of the winnings at Dover.

"Sounds like you've been reading the paper again, Mikey," Darrell said. "Don't do that. You can't believe the money you read in the newspaper. They make that amount up so the win looks bigger. The owner never gets as much as the paper says."

"Whatever." I shrugged. "Do I at least get the trophy? Or do I get a ten-percent replica of that?"

Too bad we didn't keep going. Due to sponsor conflicts, my Cup team wouldn't allow me to race Darrell's Busch car anymore. We had a deal with Mobil 1 oil, and Darrell's car was sponsored by Exxon. But I definitely didn't want to be done with Busch Series racing. I just had to find another ride.

My Cup team began entering a Busch car for me occasionally, and I did well. I won on the anniversary of my first start at Indy. I took the checkered flag in the Kroger 200 driving my Country Time car. I also sat on the pole that night. That was a nice way to celebrate an anniversary.

And I needed it. I was in Indy with a heavy heart. Emotionally, I was all over the place. Prior to the race that weekend, my mom had suffered a stroke back home in Kentucky. It was tough to stand in Victory Lane in Indianapolis and smile, knowing she was lying in a hospital bed in serious condition a few hours away. As soon as we got done in Victory Lane, Mercer and I hopped into my car and drove straight to Owensboro so I could be with Mom the next morning.

I wanted to be there with my family.

Mom's condition was stable. I spent that whole week in Kentucky, and she improved daily. It was still serious though. It was hard, but as the week came to an end, I had to head back to the races. That's what us racers do.

CHAPTER 10

GETTING FRIENDLY

Back in North Carolina, I'd been spending more and more time around Dale.

I would stop by the Busch Series shop behind his house in Moores-ville. His guys would be working on the cars, and I'd hang out with them, just trying to be one of the boys. Dale's Busch Series cars were the black #3 Goodwrench Chevys just like he raced in Cup on Sundays. The Busch Series cars were Dale's though. He was the owner. And as an owner, he was very hands-on.

Some of the time when I walked into his shop, I'd see Dale's feet hanging out from underneath a car. He'd be installing a transmission or changing a gear or whatever he might be doing up under there. But when the work was done—that was my favorite part. We might have a beer or two and tell racing stories.

The talk would generally go from racing to deer hunting or something that involved shooting a gun or a bow and arrow. That talk would then lead to target practice. Those were the first times I'd ever shot a gun. I could tell that target practice helped Dale relax. While we were shooting one night, I asked Dale if he'd let me drive his Busch car sometime.

"Darrell let me drive his, and I won," I told him.

I didn't really need to add the "I won." All I needed to say was, "Darrell let me drive his." Dale didn't want Darrell to have anything up on him.

"Yeah," he said. "You can drive it at Rockingham. And I'll pay you half of what you win."

There. It had happened again. Me getting the answer I was looking for. This was getting fun.

"Deal," I said. "Me and the black Goodwrench car." How cool would that be?

Half was about fifty percent, I figured. That was way more than the ten percent Darrell had offered up.

I couldn't wait to find Darrell and tell him about my deal with Dale. I was going to be driving for Dale Earnhardt. Not only was I going to be driving for him, but he was going to be paying me half. No more of this ten-percent B.S.

When I found Darrell, I told him, "I don't think you're aware of this, but I'm gonna be driving for Dale Earnhardt. And by the way, he's gonna be paying me fifty percent of the winnings. Not bad, huh?"

Darrell put his arm around me. "Little brother," he said, "when you get your check from Dale, you let me know which one was more—the one for a thousand dollars I gave you or the one you get from Earnhardt."

I raced hard for Dale at Rockingham that day. But I finished seventh. Seventh place in a Busch Series race in Rockingham, North Carolina, in 1989 paid $1,025. About a week later, my check from Dale showed up. Five hundred and thirteen dollars. Well, lookie there. He rounded up. I got a little more than 50 percent. But it still came up well short of the $1,000 Darrell had paid.

Big Brother was right. Darn it.

What I wouldn't give to still have Dale's check today!

That Rockingham race was my first opportunity to drive Dale's car. We tried to work it out for me to drive his car some more. And I actually did in 1994 up in Dover, Delaware, the track where I'd gotten my first Busch win driving for Darrell. But sponsor and team conflicts—again!—got in the way.

Even though I wasn't racing for him, Dale and I continued to develop something even more important: our friendship.

First it was just me, Dale, and the boys, shooting targets and racing cars. But then I started dating a girl named Buffy. Elizabeth Arrington "Buffy" Franks was the girl of my dreams, beautiful, sweet, and smart. She was a senior at the University of North Carolina at Charlotte and a part-time waitress at the Sandwich Construction Company, a local restaurant where a bunch of us racing guys all hung out. What I liked most about her was she wouldn't give me the time of day.

I was one of many racer guys competing to be in her company. She wasn't falling for me or for any of my lame friends—and our stupid boilerplate pickup lines. Lines like, "Does your heinie hurt? 'Cause it's killing me." Or, "Can I have your phone number? I lost mine."

Despite my lameness, I caught a break. When Buffy graduated from college, she got a job working at an apparel company that sold some of the drivers' licensed souvenirs. The company's star driver? Dale Earnhardt.

I had talked Dale into letting me drive his race car. That worked out pretty well. Now I wanted Dale to talk Buffy into going out with me.

Dale stepped up.

"He ain't that bad," Dale told her when he got her alone. "I hesitate to say this, but he's actually kinda smart."

"Like book-smart?" she asked.

"No way," Dale told her. "The people-smart kind. Definitely smart enough to know a good girl when he sees one."

Somehow, it must have worked.

It was 1992 when we started dating. In early 1993 I decided it was time to pop the question. We had been dating for more than six months, and we were getting along great. It was a beautiful Wednesday in April. I was lying on the couch in my condo on Lake Norman, staring out the window, watching a couple of boats float by.

The phone rang. It was my old buddy Mercer. He was in town and wanted to golf. He said, "It's beautiful out. Let's go hit 'em."

"Let me call you right back on that one, Merce," I told him.

I hung up and deliberated this decision.

Here were my options, as I saw them that day. Behind door number one: marry Buffy. I was in love with her, and I wanted to marry her. Marriage was a little scary to me, but if I was going to marry her, it was time. I needed to buy a ring and do it.

Door number two: golf with Mercer and goof off the rest of the day and maybe the rest of my life. As tempting as door number two was, I chose door number one. I called Mercer back. I told him I couldn't go golfing. I damn sure didn't tell him why, just that I couldn't. I got up off the couch and drove to Hayes Jewelers. The owner, Bruce Hayes, was a friend of Dale's. Any time I needed jewelry, he always gave me a deal.

The races that April weekend were in Bristol, Tennessee. The weather was crappy that Thursday night. So Buffy and I drove up to Bristol instead of flying. That night, Alan Kulwicki, 1992 NASCAR Winston Cup champion, died in a plane crash while trying to land at the foggy Tri-Cities Airport. Alan and I had started in NASCAR together. In 1986 we were both rookies. He won Rookie of the Year honors. I was second. Alan and I weren't friends, but we had raced together and hung around in some of the same places. I don't think we had ever had a conversation about anything significant, but his death had a real effect on me. I appreciated that the guy I had raced for Rookie of the Year honors had become a champion so quickly.

Despite Alan's death, the races had to go on. They always do. The Busch Series race was the first event after the tragedy. I won the race that day and in his honor did what Alan called his "Polish victory lap." Any time Alan would win a race—no one had ever done this before—he would take a victory lap in the opposite direction. That celebration was Alan's way of poking fun at his culture.

So that day, when I drove to Victory Lane, I did a backward lap and dedicated it to Alan. While I was being interviewed on live TV with Buffy by my side, I asked her to marry me.

ESPN commentator and former race-car driver Benny Parsons was conducting the interview.

"Are you serious, Mike?" he asked.

"Yeah," I told him. "I got the ring in the truck."

I believe Jeff Foxworthy has a line about that exact situation. "If you ask someone to marry you, but you forgot your ring in the truck, you might be a redneck."

I actually did that.

Buffy and I were married that November. The hours that Dale and I hung out in the Busch shop grew into us and our wives doing even more together. The four of us would go down to the Bahamas and spend time on the Earnhardts' boat. We would fish all day and then eat dinner together at night. Dale and Teresa's little girl, Taylor Nicole, often came with us. Sometimes, my daughter Caitlin, who was about Taylor's age, would come too. It wasn't much longer until Buffy and I had Macy. She loved the Bahamas too. When the season was finally done, Dale, Teresa, Buffy, and I would fly up to New York. We'd leave the kids at home and enjoy the big-city nightlife.

I kept going by Dale's shop just to shoot the bull with him—and sometimes targets too. It's funny though: Despite my prowess hitting targets, Dale never once asked me to go hunting with him. I always got to go fishing on the boat though. I couldn't figure out why I didn't get to go hunting too. I came up with two possible explanations. Either he didn't like the thought of me walking beside him carrying a loaded gun, or he couldn't figure out a way to convince Buffy to wear a bikini in the woods.

I liked being on the boat better anyway. So who cares?

As we spent more time together, our conversations kept getting deeper. Instead of talking about fights at the dirt track, which we still sometimes did, we talked more about kids and family and losing loved ones. We talked about the things we cared about.

When we would talk about me and racing, Dale always said the same thing: "You can win in Cup," he'd tell me. "I know you can. I can make you a winner. Maybe one day you'll drive for me."

"I hope so," I told him.

I would do anything for that chance. I'd do anything to prove him right.

CHAPTER 11

O-FER

For a guy who wasn't winning races, I sure had a lot to smile about. If you graphed the first eleven years of my Cup driving career, from 1985, when I made my first start, to 1996, the line actually sloped up.

That's kind of strange to say for someone who'd lost as many races as I had. But when I started off on Dick Bahre's team, neither one of us had much experience in the NASCAR world. We had even less money. And I'd been driving those stupid little four-cylinder cars. In no way were they anything like Cup cars. Less power, less weight, shorter wheel base—everything was different. I'm sure glad I wound up on Richard Petty's couch when I did, or no telling how many years I'd have wasted.

But with Dick in 1985 and '86, I was gaining experience in the right kind of cars. In '87, I had some competitive runs. I started making progress. In '88, a little more progress. We still didn't have the funds to build the fastest cars in the garage. But I was patiently learning my craft. With my head down, I kept on making progress.

In 1991, I won two poles in Cup, my first two. Then I earned a spot in the All-Star event by winning the qualifying race for nonwinners. I was definitely the best of them by then. I'm sure I had at least progressed from beginner to mediocre—maybe even better than that.

By then, I was getting so close, I could almost taste my first Cup victory. So close . . . Twice, early in '91, I had the best car on the track, once in Atlanta, then again a couple of weeks later in Darlington. We led both events. At Darlington, we led the most laps. Late in the race, it looked like I had a sure victory at the track Too Tough to Tame. Well, I had it tamed that day. Unfortunately, my pit crew didn't. The last stop of the day, the one I needed, was a disaster. What should have taken about fifteen seconds ended up taking forty or so. I sat there helplessly as my team struggled and the win slipped away. I ended up finishing third.

All the way through '91, we were contending and competing and doing well. I felt like it would just be a matter of time till I would be pulling into Victory Lane as a Cup winner, just like I had done in every other form of racing. But it never happened.

Nineteen ninety-two started off strong, too. I was running second in the Daytona 500 with just five laps to go when a blown engine took away my chance of winning. I had a couple of engine failures early in that season and our performance trailed off from there.

In '93, '94, and '95, we did well, finishing twelfth in the points two out of three of those seasons. Very competitive? Sure. Also for sure: no wins.

People definitely noticed. "No wins . . . no wins"—that's all the media wanted to talk about.

"Ten years . . . three hundred races . . . no wins."

It was something I couldn't hide from. All you had to do was look at the record. It was right there in black and white. That stupid zero kept getting bigger and bigger. I was doing something right, I suppose. The fans still seemed to like me okay. My sponsors hung around. And I always had owners wanting me to drive their cars. I'd seen drivers come into Cup all hyped up to be the next Richard Petty only to be out of NASCAR and back to their local tracks a year or two later.

If nothing else, I hung in there.

There were a few new drivers who did really well—Jeff Gordon and Bobby Labonte specifically. They started in Cup well after me. Both of them won the championship before I could win a race. This 0-fer-whatever-it-was was becoming quite a burden for me.

I'd never gone 0–3 at anything in my life, let alone 0–300. Go-karts, 1–0. Stock cars, 1–0. Busch Series? I won in my third start. This stupid losing streak was getting ridiculous.

Let me try to break it down for you.

For me the tough phase began in the upper 200s, somewhere around

0–275. I was progressing in my driving, I felt. I had other signs of encouragement. My team, my sponsors—they were all solidly behind me. I was loving what I was doing. But still, 275, 280, 285, 290—that's a lot of races to start without a victory, even if I did have all those reasons for hope.

I'd slip in an occasional Busch Series win here and there. Still, I'd hear all the talk.

"You think he'll ever win one?" someone would wonder.

"That's an awful long losing streak."

"Has anyone ever lost that many?"

If I were a boxer, I'd have definitely been given the standing-eight count. But I was determined not to let my record get me down. Another driver might have given up. Not me. Despite the 0-fer record, I believed it was just a matter of time. I'd get a win one day.

I'd amassed this long record of futility while driving for the same team, though the name had changed. Dick Bahre Racing was now BAHARI Racing. Two businessmen, Lowrance Harry and Chuck Rider, had bought the majority of Dick Bahre's team, and they were now calling the shots. BAHARI was a combination of the first two letters of each man's last name.

But by the middle of 1995, for the first time ever, I began hearing rumors that I was about to get canned. My performance in '95 was solid, but it looked like the Curse of the 0-fer was about to take me down.

My losing streak was approaching 300 by then. There were some other factors too. The owners of BAHARI Racing supposedly had their eye on a young hotshot driver named Johnny Benson Jr. How young? Not quite two months younger than me. That must have been a hell of a couple of months!

JB was on his way to winning the NASCAR Busch Series championship in 1995. He appeared to be the real deal. Pennzoil was our sponsor, and the man who was running Pennzoil when the company started sponsoring me, Jim Pate, had retired. Jim had become a good friend of mine. But now there was a new management team in charge, and none of them were my friends. They were putting pressure on BAHARI Racing to produce some wins.

Chuck Rider told them: "Johnny Benson Jr. will be a star in NASCAR. Johnny will take BAHARI Racing and Pennzoil to the championship table in New York City." And Pennzoil bought it.

History shows this wasn't exactly correct, but I'm sure it sounded good at the time.

Dale and I were talking one day, and I told him what I was hearing. "What do you think I should do?" I asked him.

He didn't seem too worried for me. "Somebody will want you to drive their car," he said. "I got an idea. Let me get back with you."

Which he did after a couple of days.

"Yeah," he told me, "you're getting fired. They're kicking you out at the end of the year. They're putting Benson in your car."

Well, I'll be darned! He knew way more than me about what was going on. "Do you have any idea when they'll actually tell *me* this?" I did have a contract for the '96 season, which I planned on honoring.

"Don't worry about it," Dale said. "I got you a better ride anyway. Go up there and talk to Eddie and Len."

The Wood brothers. One of the most famous teams in NASCAR, and Dale's endorsement got me the ride.

Sound familiar? His endorsement also got me my first date with my wife. And he got me a new Cup opportunity with a legendary winning team.

Before I went to speak with them, I made a point of brushing up on my Wood Brothers history. Wood Brothers Racing went all the way back to 1950. Glen and Leonard Wood came from Stuart, Virginia, in the Blue Ridge Mountains in the southwestern part of the state. They worked full-time preparing the cars, while three other Wood brothers pitched in on nights and weekends.

In addition to being famous for winning races, Wood Brothers are given credit for inventing the modern pit stop. In the early days of racing, it wasn't uncommon for a driver to pull into the pit, turn off his engine, get out, and smoke a cigarette while the crew serviced the car. Wood Brothers recognized there were races to be won by reducing the off-track time.

Sounds kind of obvious now, right? That's how Ricky Bobby got his chance.

Wood Brothers Racing's Ford carried the #21, and that number became as notorious in NASCAR as Richard Petty's #43 and Dale's #3.

Some of the greats drove for Wood Brothers—Dan Gurney, Donnie Allison, A.J. Foyt, David Pearson, Neil Bonnett, my buddy Kyle Petty—but the team's real NASCAR dominance came in the 1970s.

David Pearson signed on to drive the #21 Ford. It was one of the most successful strings of victories in motorsports history. In only seven years, from 1972 to 1979, Wood Brothers entered 143 races, winning a staggering 46 victories and 51 pole positions.

Also in the '70s, Glen Wood's sons, Eddie and Len Wood, began to take a more active role on the team. By the time I met with them, Len and Eddie were making all the calls. They were the ones who'd talked with Dale about hiring me.

I first met with Eddie and Len in mid-September. Eddie did all the talking. We agreed to the contractual terms of the deal in about two minutes. It was, "This is what it pays, this is how long we want you to do it, and you pretty much have to do what Citgo, our sponsor, wants you to."

About all I said was: "Check. Check. Check. Gotcha!"

A couple of weeks later, when it came time to sign my contract we were at the track in North Wilkesboro, North Carolina. I found Dale in the garage and asked him if he could come down to the Wood Brothers trailer and witness us signing the contract.

That seemed only right. Dale was the guy who put me and the Wood brothers together. He belonged at the signing party. This signing party was held in the back of a tractor-trailer used to haul cars around. That's how we used to do it in NASCAR.

Just like that, it was official. In 1996, I would be driving the famous #21 Wood Brothers Ford in the NASCAR Winston Cup Series.

Mikey just got another upgrade.

CHAPTER 12

ALL-STAR

When Wood Brothers decided to hand over the famous family ride
to me, I was honored—and a bit nervous. Their car was a big
part of NASCAR Winston Cup history. When I took over behind the
wheel, the #21 had been to Victory Lane ninety-six times.

I *had* to get the Woods their ninety-seventh.

It had been a few years since they had been to Victory Lane, and we
all know about my sterling record.

The '96 season started off well. By the time we got to Charlotte in
May, I'd had some really strong runs—four top tens and a top five at
Talladega. But ever since the season started, I'd had Charlotte circled on
my calendar. I had it circled because the Charlotte Motor Speedway was
my favorite track, and it was a track Wood Brothers had experienced a
lot of success on over the years.

We spend two weeks racing at Charlotte. The first weekend is the All-
Star Race. That's followed the next week by the Coke 600 (once known
as the World 600), the same race I'd run in my NASCAR Cup debut in
1985. When I got to Charlotte for All-Star weekend, Wood Brothers and
I weren't qualified for the All-Star Race. That meant we had to run the
All-Star qualifying race, which was held just prior to the big event.

To secure a transfer spot, you had to finish in the top five in the
qualifying race. That sounds easy enough, right? It's a bunch of people
who haven't won. Surely I could qualify, considering how well I'd run up
to that point in my new ride. When I headed to Charlotte, I assumed it
was a given.

You know what often happens—right?—when you make assumptions. It looked like that was about to happen to me. I was barely hanging on to the fifth position. The guy in sixth was all over me, trying to grab the last transfer spot. That guy? The next NASCAR superstar, Johnny Benson Jr. The young phenom was all over my old tail.

Wow! I was finding it hard to overcome that crucial two-month difference in our age.

With just a few laps to go and the young lion all over me, I changed my line down in turns three and four as a last-ditch effort to hold onto the all-important fifth position. And it worked. Using my new line, I pulled away from Johnny and finished fifth. That meant I would start twentieth, last in the All-Star Race. But I was in. I leaned on the two months of experience I had over Johnny, and I grabbed the last spot in the show. I had turned the young cub away.

After the qualifying race, we had about a half hour to make adjustments and be ready to start the All-Star event. I explained to Eddie and Len that the car was a mess. We needed some major chassis adjustments to get in the game. My Wood Brothers crew went to work. A couple springs, a couple shocks, and a sway bar change. We were ready to start from the back of the field for one of the biggest events of the NASCAR season.

It was a big deal to be a part of the All-Star Race. All the great teams were in it. Wood Brothers had always been one of NASCAR's elite teams. I was relieved I'd been able to put them back in the company where they belonged.

When I say All-Star event, don't get confused. This isn't like the all-star games in Major League Baseball or the NBA. This isn't just dancing around having fun. This is a serious car race. At over 190 miles an hour. People can get hurt. And the All-Star Race has one of the largest purses in all of racing. Some crazy stuff goes down when that much money is involved.

When the green flag flew and we headed into turn one, I could tell right away the adjustments my guys had made were right on. I needed some major changes. I got them. Now I could really race.

The All-Star Race is run in three segments. After the first segment, they turn the field upside down. So if you win the first segment, you start last in the second—and last starts first. I began the night from the back. One might think, why not just stay there? That would have meant I'd start first in the next segment. But I didn't like that strategy. I believed I needed to push my car as hard as I could to see what I had. If I just simply rode in the back, I wouldn't have known what to do to the car when we got a chance to make adjustments. So I charged. I made it halfway through the field in the first segment and finished tenth.

I got a couple of reminders over the radio along the way from Eddie Wood about what I was doing. "You know, if you pass those guys, you're just gonna have to pass 'em back," he said. And one of the guys I passed in that segment was Dale Earnhardt.

After the break, the field was inverted. I finished tenth, so I started segment two eleventh. Dale was just ahead of me in eighth. During the next segment, he and I both charged to the front. Dale won the second segment and I finished fourth. Now it was time for a pit stop and a ten-lap shootout to see who would win one of the biggest races of the year and the two hundred grand that went along with it.

After the second and final break, it was time to come to the green. The cream had risen to the top. Three Cup champions—Dale Earnhardt, Rusty Wallace, and Terry Labonte—lined up one, two, three. There I sat, right behind them, me and all my wins—strike that, I didn't have any of those. But I was lined up fourth. Do you think I was a bit overmatched? Yeah, me too. A little. The only thing that stood between me and victory were three of the best NASCAR drivers ever, three Hall-of-Famers for sure.

But you know why they have the races? Because in sports, you never know what's going to happen. And I can guarantee you, that was certainly true that night.

On the second lap of the ten-lap sprint to the checkered flag, I cleared Rusty and was right on the bumpers of Terry and Dale. They were side by side as we dove into turn one, when Dale's car slipped up the track. He and Terry rubbed. I cut to the bottom and drove off turn two with the lead.

A lead I never relinquished.

I beat all those champions and won NASCAR's All-Star Race.

The Woods and I had done it.

. . . .

I had finally won, and it was the All-Star Race. After so many losses, I could finally celebrate being a Cup winner.

"Michael Waltrip Passes Rusty Wallace, Terry Labonte, and Dale Earnhardt in the Final Ten Laps to Win the All-Star Race!" If someone had written that headline before the race was over, the editor would have been fired for sure.

But this win was real.

As I rode toward Victory Lane, I was thinking just how good it felt. I wanted to win for Wood Brothers more than I wanted to win for me. The #21 car now had 97 wins. This was my first. We were all going to enjoy it.

I pulled into Victory Lane, climbed out of the car, jumped onto the roof, threw my arms in the air, and saluted the fans.

Fireworks were going off above me. I'd beaten the best of the best in NASCAR on one of the biggest nights of the year. And I did it for the Wood brothers. Eddie, Len, Glen, and Leonard all flashed smiles that were priceless. These boys hadn't been to Victory Lane for a few years. Man, I was so glad I was able to take them back there.

As I stood on top of the car with all the accolades of the fans showering down on me, and me feeling so good about what I had accomplished, I thought, "This is big. Finally, no more 0-fer. I am a winner."

Or was I?

It hit me harder than I had ever hit any concrete wall. My arms still in the air and a huge smile still on my face, I thought: This doesn't count.

"It don't count."

I didn't allow the smile to fade from my face, but my feelings of joy faded. I hadn't changed a thing. I was still that same person, the 0-fer guy. Isn't that crazy? I was the All-Star champ. But all it got me in the record book was an asterisk.

You see, like in other major sports, the All-Star Race is a special event. The results of it don't count in the official record book.

Oh, you might get rich. Or you might get hurt. But either way it doesn't count.

I don't think anyone else in Victory Lane or anyone I had beaten on the track—or even the fans probably—really cared that it didn't count.

But not a single one of them were 0-fer-300. I was the only one with that special distinction.

So with a smile on my face, I climbed off the car and Glenn Jarrett from TNT television was there to interview me. Glenn, a former racer himself, looked at me and said: "What a night, Mike. What a night. How does it feel to be here in Victory Lane with the Wood brothers?"

I answered that it was a big event. It was a huge night for Citgo and Klaussner Furniture. I said all the things a driver's supposed to say, the God, Goody's, and Goodyear speech I'd learned from DW.

"Glenn," I said, "I'm gonna build my mom and dad a house. I've been wanting them to move to North Carolina. This'll pay for their house."

I got a little excited there for a second and forgot about what I knew was coming next. I could have lip-synched Glenn's next question. He said: "Mike, after all this time, a big win like this, but it's not an official points race."

"I know, Glenn. It don't count."

Other than Glenn, no one else in Victory Lane cared if it counted or not. We were just living it up. Partying on a Saturday night in Charlotte.

This win validated the Woods' hiring me. And I needed that. I didn't want to let them down. I could tell by the way they were looking: There wasn't anybody in the world they would rather have driving their car than me.

While I was celebrating with Wood Brothers and my whole team, Dale came by Victory Lane to say congratulations. He had put me and the Woods together. He knew what a big deal it was for us to win one of the biggest races of the year. My brother Darrell came as well to give me a hug. Both Dale and Darrell had won the All-Star Race. Darrell and I are the only brothers to ever win that event.

My first win with Wood Brothers, the win that didn't count, was my last win with them. At least I got them one.

Sorta.

CHAPTER 13

HELPING DAD

When I won the All-Star race in 1996, I said in Victory Lane that I was going to build my parents a house with all the money I'd won.

Mom and Dad still lived back in Owensboro, Kentucky. I wanted them to move to Sherrills Ford, North Carolina, and be neighbors to Buffy and me. We lived out in the country and had plenty of room to build them a place they'd be proud of. Mom and Dad were into it. They wanted to move. We were excited and began working right away on their house.

Before the house was finished and Mom and Dad could move down, my dad was diagnosed with lung cancer. We were sad, but Dad was ready to fight. He began his treatment in Owensboro and told us to keep building their house in North Carolina. I loved my dad's attitude. "We're going to beat this cancer, Pop," I told him. Buffy and I were researching where we could get the best care for him.

We talked to Rick Hendrick, a NASCAR team owner and a friend of the family who was fighting cancer himself. I asked Rick about the doctors who were treating him. He put me in touch with them, and they suggested we take Dad to the University of Kentucky. The team at UK could make a plan for treating Dad and hopefully cure his lung cancer. Not only were Dad's doctors some of the best in their field, UK was a short drive from Owensboro. And all the Waltrips were big University of Kentucky Wildcats fans. So in addition to the care Dad would receive, he thought it was cool he was being treated at the university.

We had it all set up. When Mom and Dad moved to North Carolina in late 1996, the team at UK handed Dad off to the same doctors who were successfully treating Rick. They then began treating Dad. Dad's spirit was strong. His attitude was amazing. And man, was he ever proud of me.

"You got me the best doctors in the world, son," he would say. "These are the doctors who cured Rick. I know they're gonna cure me too."

And it was a good thing Dad had such a positive attitude. The chemo and radiation were hard on him. Dad was in his seventies, and he'd had a rough year. Before the treatment for cancer could begin, Dad had to have heart surgery. He had a leaky aortic valve that needed to be replaced. They'd performed the operation in Owensboro, and it was a success. The replacement valve came from a pig. Dad liked the fact that he had a piece of a pig in his heart. He would always say, "That ol' pig is pumping away in there. She's doing her job."

Once Dad recovered from the heart surgery, we started our trips to the University of Kentucky for his cancer treatments. Every time I showed up to take him for treatment, he would always be standing there waiting for me with a positive attitude, all dressed up and ready to go. He loved me being there for him. He was confident we were going to beat this thing together. We were a team. We were going to win.

After Mom and Dad moved to North Carolina, we wanted Dad to maintain his zest for life. Despite the fight against cancer, this was a special time for me and my dad. A typical day for us would begin with Dad's treatment. Then we'd have lunch and maybe even play golf if he felt like it. Sometimes, Dad would go to the races with us. I always wanted him to be looking forward to something.

One day at lunch I asked Dad if he wanted to go on vacation. "Tell me where you want to go, and we'll plan it," I said.

Dad said he'd always wanted to take Mom to Hawaii. "Can we go there?" he asked.

"Hawaii it is," I announced.

That was November 1998. If you had a picture of our group in Hawaii, you would definitely have laughed. We brought Macy, our baby girl, who had just celebrated her first birthday. So we had her stroller. Mom was there. She couldn't get along very well at all because of her stroke. So we had her crutches. Dad was battling cancer. He needed a lot of help. There we were, all of us, laid up on the beach in Hawaii, coconut drinks in our hands, complete with frilly umbrellas. I really appreciated Buffy signing up for that trip with the in-laws. It was a challenge, but oh, so worth it.

Dad loved being able to show Mom Hawaii, and Mom loved being there. I just loved that everybody was feeling so much love.

Who doesn't love love?

It was so special for me to see those two enjoying life. After Hawaii, we stopped in San Francisco for a couple of days. Dad had been stationed there in World War II, and he wanted to visit the base where he'd lived.

The next summer, I was always doing something with Dad. One of the things we enjoyed the most was going to the Bristol races in August. The North Carolina mountains sit between Sherrills Ford and Bristol, Tennessee. Dad loved going to the mountains to golf. This was a guys' trip for us. It is always as hot as Hades in Sherrills Ford in August. But about seventy miles away and a mile up, the mountain air is cool and fresh. Our last trip there was in 1999.

We arrived late on a Tuesday evening. We always stayed with our friend, Knox Hillman, God rest his soul.

Knox had a condo overlooking the golf course where we played. Early Wednesday morning, just as the sun began peeking through my bedroom window, I could already hear Dad in the kitchen making coffee.

It got quiet after a few minutes, so I got up to check on him. What I saw made me really happy. There was Dad, standing on the balcony of the condo with a cup of coffee in his hand. He was already dressed; my dad always liked to look good.

There were times when he wouldn't exactly match right. I'd even seen him accidentally wear one black shoe and one brown shoe. Not this time. He was looking sharp. If you'd seen him, you'd have thought he just stepped out of a Sears catalogue. He was wearing a pair of light-brown cotton pants and a burgundy plaid polo shirt. He was looking fine and ready to golf.

Knox's condo had a great view of the course. Looking down from the balcony, you could see the well-manicured fairways and the picturesque mountains that surrounded the area and helped to frame the course.

It was a fabulous morning that Wednesday. The dew was still shimmering on the grass as the sun began shining over the mountaintops. As Dad stood there, leaning slightly over the railing with his coffee, I just watched. I tried to imagine what my daddy was thinking. I wondered if he was saying to himself: "This is why I'm going to beat cancer." Or maybe it was just, "Thank you, Lord. Every day's a gift."

After a few minutes of observing Dad, I walked up from behind, put my arm around his shoulder, and said: "It's something, isn't it, Pops? What do you think?"

His response was 100-percent Leroy. "I will bet you, son," he said, "I will bet you they make us stay on them damn cart paths."

If you ever wanted to know what Dad was thinking, all you had to do was ask.

I was thinking the reply I would get would be, "It's beautiful." Or perhaps, "I just saw a deer walk by." I certainly didn't see the cart path comment coming. Because the place was so beautiful, Dad was afraid we'd have to stay on the cart path instead of driving up to wherever he hit his ball. He wasn't up to walking all over the place.

I quickly reassured him. "We don't have to stay on those paths, Dad," I told him. "I'll get us one of those orange flags."

Sometimes golf courses give orange flags to golfers who are older or physically challenged. And with an orange flag, you can drive anywhere on the course.

Dad smiled.

"You can get me one of those flags that old people have on their carts?" he asked. "You can do that, son?"

"Yes, Dad," I told him. "For you, I can. I will get us a flag."

Dad shook his head in amazement. "You're the best."

After a couple of days of golfing it was time to go to Bristol. We had really enjoyed the mountains, but it was time to get back to business, the business of racing. The Bristol Motor Speedway is one of the most challenging tracks in all of NASCAR. It's a high-banked speed bowl, a half-mile track that we cover in just over fifteen seconds a lap. They call it the "Concrete Cage." Racing there is like flying jet fighters in a gymnasium.

My point is things happen in a hurry in Bristol. Quite a transition from the tranquil setting of a golf course in the mountains to what amounts to 130-mile-per-hour car wrestling. And I loved them both.

The first race in Bristol that weekend was the Friday night Busch Series match, a 250-lapper. I was racing hard that night, and as the laps wound down, I was closing on the leader and thought I was going to win. What a great way to finish up my special trip with Dad! I wanted to win so bad. But I didn't. And it pissed me off.

When the checkered flag fell with Dad watching from the suites, I ended up second. Oh, so close! Why? Why, God? Why couldn't you let me win this one for Dad?

For a racer, there is no bigger gap than the one from first to second. The difference between third, fourth, seventh, or eleventh is not nearly as big a deal. But second place is the first loser, and it always will be.

I wanted to win for him so badly. Why couldn't God see that my dad needed to celebrate that night? I couldn't imagine he'd have many more chances to do so. In fact, I didn't even know if he would ever get to see another race in person. My last win was in the All-Star Race back in 1996, more than three years earlier. And on that night in Bristol, I was right there. I could taste it.

When the race was over, I wondered what my dad was thinking. I got beat. Sure, I finished second. My team and my sponsors were proud. But I bet Dad would be disappointed I couldn't grab that checkered flag for him.

To win would have been the icing on the cake after our special week.

But blaming God for me not winning—that was an emotional reaction. Dumb, too. And selfish.

Heck, it was a car race. And a great car race. Matt Kenseth beat me. He was just faster. It wasn't like a cruel twist of fate took the win from me. I just got outrun.

Grow up, you butt!

When I saw Dad after the race, I felt even dumber about questioning

God. Dad was all smiles. "You almost won, son," he said excitedly. "That was a great race, and you did an amazing job. You about beat that dude."

Dad was really happy and that made me feel better—and worse. Happy over Dad's joy. Guilty over my "Why, God?" attitude.

I hate when I question God's grace and mercy. I don't have any answers. Who do I think I am?

CHAPTER 14

PUSHING DAD

As fall settled in on North Carolina, I could tell Dad's days of feeling like golfing—or generally just goofing off—were becoming fewer and farther between. Most every day, I would go over to his and Mom's and see what he was up to. I'd find out if he wanted to do anything or just hang around.

More often than not, Dad was pretty content to just lie in his chair and watch TV.

We would still have to go to the hospital occasionally for breathing treatments or maybe even radiation. But that more or less was the extent of our going or doing. Occasionally, I could talk him into going to lunch or dinner but not very often. We hadn't golfed since we were in the mountains before Bristol.

One beautiful day in Sherrills Ford, I decided to spread some fertilizer on one of the fields next to my house. This is another one of my favorite Leroy stories. I was on my tractor, driving from one end of the field to the other. As I made a pass, I looked over and saw my dad driving down the driveway. That was a bit strange, I thought, because Dad hadn't been getting out much. But as he drove by, I waved. I figured he was just headed to the Busch shop to check on the guys.

I was really happy he was out.

He used to hang around the race shop a lot. He would go see what the boys were working on. We had a big race coming up in a couple of weeks in Charlotte, and I figured he was going down to make sure everyone knew he planned on being there and that he expected us to win.

Dad and I could both taste victory at Bristol when we were there. So I'm sure he thought that a little encouragement from the patriarch of the Waltrip family would be enough to push us over the top.

But Dad didn't stop at the shop. He turned right around. I kept one eye on the field I was fertilizing and one eye on Dad.

What was he doing?, I wondered as I came back toward the shop.

Dad had stopped his car on the driveway. He got out of the car and simply waved at me as I tractored on by. When I made the turn this time and headed back toward Dad, I loved what I saw. Dad had gotten into the trunk of his car and pulled out a golf club and was waving it at me.

Ha, ha! Dad was wanting to golf. How cool was that?

I was being summoned to his car with what looked like a three wood, and straight to his car I went. I parked my tractor, jumped off, and said: "You wantin' to golf, Dad?"

"Yes, son. That's what I was hoping we could do."

"We can do anything you like, Dad. Let me put on my golfing clothes, and we'll be right on our way."

Times like these with my dad were very important to me. I felt like it was almost role reversal for me. I was acting like the dad, and Dad was the needy child. Most of the time as a kid, when I was that needy child, Dad wasn't around. But kids are tough. They learn how to deal with things. Dad wasn't tough anymore. I wasn't about to let him down when he needed me.

Although golfing was rare and Dad was getting weaker, he was able to make the Charlotte race, just like he'd promised the boys in the shop. Our house in Sherrills Ford is about a forty-five-minute drive from the Charlotte Motor Speedway. I talked Mom into coming with Dad to the race that day.

All tracks these days have luxury suites above the grandstand where sponsors can entertain their customers. I'd gotten Mom and Dad passes for a suite so they could be comfortable and see the race from a great spot.

Despite the fact that Dad had been encouraging my team about performing, the Charlotte race wasn't going as well as the one in Bristol had. My car just wasn't fast that day. I qualified in the back and was only able to make minimal gains. But as the laps wound down in the race, something crazy began to occur. The leaders all started making pit stops for fuel. One after another, the guys who were ahead of me hit Pit Road. My crew chief said he thought we could make it to the finish with the gas we had. But I would definitely be on E if we made it to the checker.

Five to go. Four to go. Three. Two. And when the white flag waved, I was still chugging along, running second, right on the bumper of the leader.

I gotta make a move, I thought. This looks a lot like Bristol. Maybe I can win this one for Dad.

As we raced off turn two, the leader went low. I decided to swing high and try to roll around the outside for the win. My move worked this time. I hit the back stretch with the lead.

What a move!

Then I glanced in my mirror and realized the great move I had made was a success because the leader that I passed had run out of gas too.

Everyone did. Except me.

With Mom and Dad looking on, I took the checkered flag and won the race. What a great day! What a gift! A gift for my sick dad! And certainly a reminder to me not to ever question God's grace like I had at Bristol.

It was another twist of fate that affected the outcome. It was a cruel twist to all those other people, the ones without gas. But to me, it was a gift.

And with my dad at the last race he would ever attend, the trophy and the checkered flag were ours. And we did it with about the tenth-best car, but the most fuel-efficient one.

Thank you, God, for allowing my dad to enjoy that win.

We had a fan-club celebration scheduled following the race. About four or five hundred fans showed up to get an autograph, eat a hot dog, and talk about racing. We had those once a year and always around the Charlotte race.

That night, the guest of honor was Mr. Leroy Waltrip. I dedicated the win to him and presented him with the winning trophy. That was a great night. That was a great way for my dad to spend his last day at the races.

A few weeks after our big win in Charlotte, we had to take Dad back to the hospital with a nasty lung infection. Infections aren't highly unusual for someone going through chemo and radiation. By that point, his immune system was beaten down pretty good. Every time we had to take Dad back to the hospital, I was afraid he would never get out.

When Dad had been in the hospital for a couple of days, he seemed to be improving after being on IVs and breathing treatments. I had spent the night with him, and he had slept really well. There was very little coughing like I had heard so many nights before. When Dad woke up, I couldn't wait to ask him: "How you feeling, Dad? Sounds like you slept really well."

"I feel great," he said.

Good, I thought. Dad's all tuned up and ready to go home.

Then Dad said: "I hope they let me out of this place today. I don't want to be here anymore. I want to go home to Momma."

"I'll tell the doctors you feel great, and you're ready to go home," I told him. "I'm sure they'll let us get out of here."

At about eleven o'clock that morning, his doctor stopped in and cleared us to leave. That's exactly what Dad wanted to hear.

We stopped at Fuddruckers on the way home and had hamburgers. We always liked stopping at Fuddruckers. It was part of our leaving-the-hospital routine. It was early afternoon, and this was shaping up to be a good day.

When I got him to his house in Sherrills Ford, he felt so good and was doing so well, I was content. I spent a few minutes catching Mom up on what the doctors had told me to expect from Dad over the next few days. There were some new medicines he would be taking. So I had to familiarize Mom with those. Mom loved being in charge of the medicines Dad had to take. She would put them in a pill box and tell him what to take and when to take them.

They seemed to be in such good shape, Mom and Dad, that I decided I was going to run over to the office. My office was right around the corner behind my house.

"I'll be back in a little while, y'all, to make sure you're doin' okay," I said.

"Okay," Dad said. "Me and Mom will be right here. We'll be fine."

When I left, I was confident that everything was under control. I didn't feel like it was necessary to ask Buffy to go watch them nor did I call my sister to go sit with them.

Dad had been in the hospital for a few days, and I could tell he was eager to visit with Mom. Dad really looked good, and he was full after his cheeseburger. I could just picture him crawling in his chair and taking a nap.

About an hour later, my phone rang. It was Mom. "Dad fell," she said. "Can you come over here and help get him up?"

I rushed to my car and over to their house. On the way, I thought: "How could you have done that? How could you have left him alone?"

I totally made a mistake by not staying with them or calling someone. Leaving them alone was dumb.

Dad didn't break any bones when he fell, but I know it broke his spirit. He really never recovered from that fall. We got him up and he was able to walk a little bit. But that fall hurt his body way more than he let any of us know. He was weak. He was in pain. And he was never the same again.

Even when I think of that day now, it hurts my heart that I let it happen. I knew his time was short and that there wasn't much chance he was ever getting better. But I wanted to keep him around as long as I could.

But when he hit the floor that day, it knocked most of the life out of him. I just wish I would have been there to catch him when he fell.

A few weeks later, in the middle of December, Dad's condition had worsened. He didn't have much energy. He didn't do much, and he really wouldn't say all that much.

I made another decision that I wish I hadn't made. This was the last one. I went over that day like I always did, and when I got there, Dad was lying in his chair.

"You all right, Dad?" I asked.

"Yeah, I'm okay, son."

"Good," I told him. "Because we got stuff we need to get done today. Get up. Get dressed. And let's go do a little bit of shopping and get a good lunch at Stacey's."

Stacey's is a neat little restaurant near our house that Dad loved going to. Everyone at Stacey's treated Dad nice. They made him feel special.

"Let's go," I said. "Get up. It'll be fun."

Dad didn't think that sounded like much fun, and he didn't hesitate to let me know. "You just don't get it, do you?" he said sharply. "How much I hurt, how much pain I'm in."

I could barely breathe. "Aw, come on, Dad. We need to go get Mom her Christmas present. Let's go see Santa."

Dad didn't laugh.

I was just trying to push him a little and encourage him. He didn't like anything I was saying. For him, that was the last straw.

"You don't even understand what I'm going through or how bad just lying here hurts," he said. "Just leave me alone."

It wasn't a very merry Christmas for us that year. Dad just lay over there in his chair very much disconnected from all that was going on around him. We brought in a nurse to sit with Dad near the end. We explained to her about Dad's day, how he could get up and come sit in his chair and she would need to help him do that. And when he needed to use the bathroom, the nurse would have to help him do that as well. We assumed Dad wasn't paying any attention to anything we were saying. But as soon as we told the nurse she would have to help him go to the bathroom, he said: "And I pee a lot."

He still had it.

That made us laugh that day, and it still does.

That was the middle of December 1999. Dad died on January 10, 2000. But really, he quit living on that day in December when I pushed him too hard. I had pushed him, all right, right over the edge. He was done fighting. I wish I hadn't done that that day. It was just too much.

That January night before Dad died, I could tell the end was near. So I helped him out of his chair, walked him to his bed, and lay down with him. As we lay there, I prayed. I asked God to tell Dad I was sorry, sorry for making him feel like I was being unfair to him at the end.

I loved him so much. And all the years of us fighting his dreadful disease together were special for us. He trusted me and believed we could win this fight.

But we didn't.

I'd been able to do so much for him—taking him to all the treatments, moving him and Mom, spending all that time together at the end, even going to Hawaii. Dad always told people how much he loved me and how much he appreciated all I had done for him and Mom. But as he lay there in my arms, struggling, taking his last breaths, I felt like I had let him down. I just closed my eyes and prayed he remembered the good times.

PART 3:
DAYTONA

CHAPTER 15

HELLO, DALE

The year 2000 started out rough for me. Happy New Year. Y2K, my butt. My dad died in my arms. *No* child should experience that. And my racing wasn't going all that great, either. Although Dale had told me many times that if I were driving for him I'd be winning, the longer I heard it, the less likely it seemed it would ever occur.

Dale's team was doing well. The part-time-behind-his-house hobby had become a full-time NASCAR operation. The little shop where I used to hang around while Dale was working on his Busch cars and we would shoot guns his guys called the Deer-Head Shop—bet you can't guess why, can you? Antlers everywhere. The Deer-Head Shop had morphed into a factory that included the old building and a couple new ones next door. Just outside Mooresville, North Carolina, on what is now called Highway 3 in Dale's honor, that compound became the headquarters of Dale Earnhardt, Inc.

Folks in NASCAR had their own name for what Dale built. They called it the Garage-Mahal. By 2000, DEI was running two NASCAR Cup Series teams and one Busch team out of this massive, ultra-modern facility in a rural part of North Carolina. And all of them were winning. Dale Junior, the two-time Busch Series champion, had moved up to Cup and was winning in his rookie season. Steve Park, Dale's other Cup driver, had won too. I completely agreed with Dale that I could be winning if I were driving one of his cars. But it didn't look like there was room for me, and another year was about to be over. It was September 2000, and I needed to make some decisions of my own about 2001. But man, I was frustrated. All these kids—first it was Gordon and Labonte, now Dale Junior and Park—showing up and getting these great rides and winning. Meanwhile, I just kept logging laps.

Nineteen-ninety-nine and 2000 were the two worst years of my career. My patience was wearing thin, that was for sure. In two years, I almost won a couple of races, but that was about it. I wasn't consistently competitive. I didn't like what I was doing.

The team I was driving for didn't operate out of a factory like Dale's. They just put the pieces together. Go down the street, buy a car. Go up the street, buy an engine. Then just bolt it all together. Anyone could have owned a team like that. Just buy parts and pieces, put them together, and go race. That's what we did behind the house in Sherrills Ford. But that was the Busch Series, which was bush league. If you wanted to win in Cup, you had to do it like Dale's team was doing: make everything.

As the 2000 season wound down, the owner of the car I was driving, Jim Smith, offered me a new contract to drive his car again the following year. There were some other possibilities out there as well. A couple of owners had interviewed me and shown interest in my plans for 2001. But none of that had firmed up yet. And none of those opportunities was remotely close to what Dale Earnhardt could offer me.

I always loved it when Dale would say, "You'd win in my car."

And I would think: Well, make it happen!

It didn't look like 2001 was a possibility. We were less than five months away from Daytona. You can't build a team that quickly, and I knew it. Looked to me like I was going to be signing a contract with a team I knew it would be nearly impossible to win with.

"I don't feel good about this, Buff," I told my wife. "I don't know what I'm gonna do. If I sign with the same team for 2001, I'll feel like I'm giving up hope of finally winning races, just signing to have a job. And I don't want to do that."

But I made my living racing cars. That's all I knew how to do. You know, the whole sitting-on-my-butt thing. I had a wife and a couple of kids, and I had to provide for them. Whatever I decided would be a compromise. My desire to win, from what I could see, would have to take a backseat to just making a living, and that made me sad. I never raced cars just to make a living. But it felt like that's what I was going to have to do then.

The truth is this had been a pattern with me, just staying with a team for stability, I suppose. I wasn't confident enough—didn't believe in myself enough to take a chance by putting myself out on the market. I'd been taking the safe route—or what seemed to be the safest bet.

But I was over that. I didn't want to just sign or settle. Not yet, anyway.

I was waiting around as long as I could, although I kept wondering why.

Tick, tick, tick. A lot of time passed and it didn't appear that one of the top rides was going to be offered to me. They never had been. Why did I think one would be now? Time kept slipping away. And I kept losing races, feeling stuck. 0–450. 0–451. I don't know how many exactly. One thing I did know, I wasn't expecting the Hall of Fame to be knocking on my door anytime soon.

Maybe I wasn't the most sought-after driver, but I was good enough that I had people calling me. I was better than most of the drivers who were available.

What was the answer? I was so confused.

My thinking about all that was interrupted by the ringing phone.

"Hello," I answered.

It was Earnhardt. "Did you sign that contract?" he demanded in that familiar tone. I laughed to myself. He was always so direct.

"No, why?"

"Well, don't," Dale said. "I'm tired of Busch racing. Makes more sense for my company to have three Cup teams. And I'm gonna fly down to Atlanta today and tell NAPA that. I'm gonna see if they want to move up to Cup, and I'm gonna tell 'em I want you to drive. I'll call you when I get back and tell you how it went."

Just that quickly he hung up.

What just happened?

I don't think I got another word in after "No, why?" It was just Dale being Dale after that, telling me what we were going to do and how we were going to do it. Just like he always did. And I loved it.

Okay.

That's a call I'd been waiting for. But I damned sure didn't see it coming. As soon as we hung up, I called Buffy and told her about Dale's call. We were both ecstatic. We knew if this came true, it would be my best chance ever to win consistently, or even at all. Maybe my last chance.

I'd be on a multicar team. Multicar teams were just beginning to become a trend in NASCAR. Owners like Dale had figured out that the more cars you had under one roof, the more cost-effective it was. For example, while a fabricator was stamping out a part or a piece in the factory for one car, he could just simply stamp out a couple more for the other cars. So if it took twenty people to build one car, maybe it only took ten more to build a second or a third—and so on. The owner then could take the money saved on the stampers and spend it on research and development or on testing to improve the team's performance.

That's a basic lesson on the modern economics of NASCAR.

Driving for my friend Dale was the opportunity I needed. He was wanting to take me under his wing at the ripe old age of thirty-seven. He wanted to show people I could win in his car. While Dale and his business guy, Ty Norris, flew down to Atlanta to meet with the NAPA people, all I could do was wait and wonder: Is my life about to change? Could Dale talk those guys into this? I figured NAPA was in for a million or two on Dale's Busch team. I knew a season with a high-profile NASCAR team like Dale's would be way more than that. And time! Was there time to do this? If so, Dale would need to know immediately in order to build the cars and hire the people.

In my mind, this sounded like a real stretch. But this was Dale Earnhardt doing the stretching. Maybe he could pull it off.

I could picture Dale in a corporate boardroom. I'd never seen him in one, but I could definitely picture him there. I wondered how he was doing at NAPA. This may have been a job that only Dale Earnhardt could tackle. He was smart. He was respected. He had a plan. And when he got there, Ty later told me, Dale was simply amazing. After a few minutes of hi-how-are-you's, Dale told the president of NAPA, "We came to talk to you guys about moving up to Cup racing with us next year."

"Next year?" one of the NAPA guys asked. "Like five months from now? Can you be ready by Daytona?"

"Not only ready. Ready to win. And I want Michael Waltrip to drive for us."

Ty wondered how it would go over. That pink-elephant thing, you know. He was wondering if they'd mention my record. But the NAPA folks didn't seem to mind.

"Can you get him?" the NAPA president asked.

"Yes, we can get him." Then Dale summarized, matter-of-factly laying out the deal: This is how it's gonna work, this is what it's gonna cost, and Michael Waltrip will drive. Then he slipped in on them at the end: "Oh, by the way, I need to know by Friday."

"Which Friday, Dale?"

"This one," Dale said. "The one in a couple days."

And with that, Dale and Ty were out the door and headed back to Mooresville.

Mike Rearden, the motorsports manager at NAPA, told me later that when Dale and Ty left the room, the company president looked at him and said, "Well, Mike, you said we should be in Cup. Sounds like Earnhardt agrees with you. You have a couple of days to present your case to me and the board."

On the plane back to North Carolina, Ty said he told Dale, "You didn't give 'em many options there, boss."

"There ain't no options," Dale said. "That's the way it's gotta work—or it won't."

When they landed, Ty called me and told me to meet Dale and him at DEI.

"You tell me, Ty. Tell me now. What happened?"

Ty told me to chill out. "It went good," he said. "But Dale wants to share the details with you. Meet us at the shop in the trophy room at seven."

I had been to DEI about a thousand times, but driving there that evening was different. My mind was in overdrive. I was thinking about what it would mean if this happened. Man, my daddy would have been so happy.

Dad was funny when he would talk about Dale. Darrell and I used to laugh at Dad. When we were at the track and Dale would drive by, every time Dad would say, "Boys, that damn Earnhardt is flying. I don't think he's even letting off in the turns." Dad would say that no matter where we were.

Dale was good, but everybody had to let off the gas for most of the turns. Whether Dale was fast or not, it didn't matter. He just looked fast to Dad.

And Mom had become a Big E fan too. She liked the fact that Dale and Teresa and Buffy and I were friends. She enjoyed hearing about the vacations we would take together. But Dale became a favorite of Mom's the day after Dad died back in January when he drove out to Sherrills Ford just to hold Mom's hand and tell her he was thinking about her. That was special to everyone in our whole family because it meant so much to Mom.

I was thinking, "If I go home and tell my momma I'm gonna drive for Dale Earnhardt, she's gonna have a fit!"

And what about me? This was what I needed, and what I'd wanted for years. I couldn't wait.

So as I pulled up to the Garage-Mahal, it felt different this time. Oh, did it look mighty! Is this where they'll build my cars? I wondered. My cars, being built in a factory, not just being bolted together somewhere. It felt like a dream.

I went around to the back and up to Dale's private entrance like I always did. Up the stairs and into a hallway that opened into the waiting room just outside Dale's and Teresa's offices. It also led to the trophy room.

The interior of the DEI headquarters was just as impressive as the exterior. Other than walking past a display of Dale's trophies, you'd never know you were in the same building where they were building a bunch of race cars. The walk to the trophy room took you across a marble floor. The chairs were covered in fine leather. And I'd eaten there before too. The chef was world-class and he prepared health-conscious food. And they also had a mighty fine wine list.

When I walked in, there Dale sat, in the same place he always did, his favorite chair. When I said, "Hey," the grin on his face got bigger.

"You ready to win some races?" he asked.

"Are we going racing?" I didn't give him a chance to answer. "All right! This will be so cool!"

"Hold! Hold! Calm down there. NAPA didn't commit yet. They need a few days."

What! I thought but didn't say out loud. Don't do that, you teaser. "A few days"? What's "a few" to Dale?

Then Dale started explaining to me how the deal would work if NAPA were to commit. Like he needed to, I thought. It would be just like it was with the Wood boys. "Just tell me what I gotta do and—check, check, check." You think I was going to sit there and negotiate with Dale Earnhardt?

But he seemed to be into telling me about the terms of the deal, like the length of the contract, how much he was going to pay me, what I had to do—all the things that Dale as the owner felt like he needed to explain to me.

In my mind all of that was just a formality until he said: "And we'll know by Friday."

What's today? I asked myself. It's Tuesday. Friday seems like forever. That's three days of wandering around with my future hanging in the balance.

Would I have to take a ride just to make a living for my family? Or would I be able to drive a car I could win with? The frustrating part was that the decision would be made in Atlanta. All I could do now was pray. And hope.

But now I had hope.

CHAPTER 16

THE DECISION

Three days. Just three days. That doesn't sound like such a long time. When I hear three days, I think about Jesus and all that went down for him in three days. I knew my life might be very different after these three days. I had fifteen years of history to overcome. Fifteen years of trying too hard and coming up short. After fifteen years, people in the NASCAR world knew me better for what I hadn't accomplished than for what I had.

The first day of waiting for NAPA's decision wasn't all that bad. Dale's optimism in the trophy room was still all over me. It was like Ricardo Montalban was standing there and had just said, "Welcome to Fantasy Island." And the dwarf, Tattoo, agreed. Dale was confident. Why shouldn't I be?

But day two was a different story. I did not like day two at all.

It began with me obsessing over what was going on in Atlanta where the decision was being made. All the different scenarios were playing in my mind.

I hope the people down there know what a big deal this is to me, I was thinking. I feel like getting in my car right now, driving down there and telling 'em. I wonder if they know I've never gone three races in anything I've ever started without winning except for Cup. I could tell 'em this 0-for-four-hundred-and-whatever start I'm off to, it must be some kind of mistake. I know what I'd say: I've never lost one race driving for Dale's team—or for you—and maybe you guys should focus on that. But they'd probably tell me they know what they have to do to sell auto parts, and they appreciate my input, but could I please leave now so they can continue their research.

This waiting was nerve-wracking and exhausting. Then I started thinking what a big disaster a "Thanks but no thanks" from NAPA would mean for me.

I didn't want to just fade away as a footnote in NASCAR history—a guy who may have lost more races than anyone in Cup. I wanted to change that. I wanted to be a winner. I couldn't stand the thought of how the Waltrip family history would read after NAPA's "No, thanks": One brother, eighty-four wins, three championships. The other brother, zero and zero.

Sure, I was the sweeter, taller, and better-looking brother, but they don't put that in the record books. A-holes!

This career that had started with such promise could soon be ending in disappointment. Day two was dark. I couldn't wait for it to end. It did.

Day three was Friday, decision day. I woke up in Richmond, Virginia, where that weekend's NASCAR races were being held.

Day three could be a whole lot better, I knew—or a whole lot worse. Or the news from Atlanta could be: "We need three more days, Dale." That would be better than an outright no, but how much better? Dale had made it clear he needed to know by Friday.

And he didn't just make Friday up. That's when he *had* to know by in order to get ready for Daytona.

When I got out of bed in my bus at Richmond International Raceway, I knew that this most likely would be the day I'd find out what my future looked like.

Would I just continue to be the so-so race-car driver laboring and hoping I'd win because everybody else ran out of gas like they did in Charlotte when I won for my dad? There could be worse things, I told myself. You can't win if you're not out there trying.

It looked like I'd be able to do something in 2001. But I didn't want to do just something. I wanted to race for Dale. With that opportunity, I could define my career.

Come on, you bunch of folks down there in Atlanta who I don't even know! Come on, NAPA! Come through!

Fortunately for me, being at Richmond meant being at the racetrack.

Nothing takes your mind off the outside world like strapping yourself into a seven-hundred-horsepower race car. That'll grab your attention. For me, most of that Friday I knew I'd be focused on the race and my car.

After making a couple of practice runs, I looked up and Dale was walking toward me. He leaned in and asked how I was doing. I went right into telling him about my car.

"I can't get it to turn," I said. "And when it does, the back end won't stay under me. Same old stuff you fight at Richmond."

Typical racer-to-racer chatter. But Dale didn't come over to ask me about my car, and I think it's funny that I didn't realize that. Dale had come to tell me NAPA had called.

But I was making it hard for him to deliver the news. Before he could get around to telling me what he'd come over for, I asked him: "What's your car doing?"

"Which one of mine?" he asked. "The one I drive, or the ones I own?"

Then suddenly it struck me: Oh, yeah. He does own cars. And it's Friday, NAPA day. I forgot. How could I do that? "Right. Your cars. Am I gonna be driving one of them next year?"

He nodded and then gave me that big Earnhardt grin. "Yep. NAPA is in. I'm going to race three Cup teams next year."

"Well, congratulations, car owner," I told him.

"You too, driver."

Do you know how many guys in the world would want to be addressed by Dale Earnhardt like that?

"Driver."

That's who I'd just become, the one-in-a-million guy.

I wanted to jump for joy. And I tried to do so, and to grab Dale too. But I was strapped in. I could barely pump my fists. But I was happy. Another answer I wanted to hear.

The crazy thing was, I couldn't tell anybody. It wasn't like I could push the radio button and tell my current team that Dale Earnhardt and NAPA had just hired me. After all, I was in Richmond to race for their team.

So when Dale walked off, I just had to sit there. All by myself. On Fantasy Island.

But I wanted to tell somebody. I couldn't wait for practice to be over. In fact, I couldn't wait for the weekend to be over, for the season to be over. I didn't give up on the rest of the 2000 season. But the races I most looked forward to were the ones coming up in 2001, the ones I'd be racing in for Dale Earnhardt, Inc.

The person I wanted to tell first was Buffy. She was waiting in the bus. She was as nervous as I was to learn the answer from NAPA. So when I got out of the car, I went straight to the bus. We high-fived like you see on TV. Then I told her, "We gotta call Momma." We did, and Mom couldn't believe it. After sharing the news with my family, it was time to share it with the NAPA family.

To do that, Dale and I headed west aboard N1DE, his Learjet, to attend a big NAPA convention in Las Vegas. It was going to be a quick trip: We left Statesville Wednesday around noon and would return there twelve hours later, after spending six or seven hours in the air and a few more with the NAPA folks in Vegas.

When we got to Vegas, Dale introduced me to the NAPA family as his "next winning driver." Me, the driver of the new NAPA #15 car.

Back on the jet heading east, you probably would have thought we'd sleep or just relax. But that wasn't how Dale rolled. He liked to play gin rummy. The game was Rummy 500; the first to get to five hundred points won. That could take a while.

Three hours and twenty minutes later when we landed in Statesville, the score was 640 to 620. The game went into overtime. You see, I was leading when we got to five hundred, but not by much, and Dale said I had to win by twenty points. And by the time we got off the plane he had beaten me.

I'd told Buffy. Buffy and I told Momma. Dale and I told NAPA. Now it was time to tell the world. We needed to hurry up and do the telling.

We wanted the announcement to have a little drama. But keeping secrets in the NASCAR world is never easy. There's people you have to tell. If you're starting a team, you have to let your team know. You'll need a sponsor. You have to tell your sponsor your plan. You have to hire people. They'll want to know what they'll be working on. Sometimes, by the time you get around to the formal announcement, everybody already knows.

Whether everybody knew what Dale was going to announce or not, they wanted to hear him explain—not what he was doing but why he was doing it. So when Dale and Teresa announced a press conference at DEI headquarters, there was a huge turnout.

I drove up in a NAPA delivery truck with a giant blue-and-yellow hat on top of it.

I didn't so much mind the first question that was asked. I just didn't like how it was asked.

"Why Michael?" one of the reporters asked in a tone that was nowhere close to flattering.

Dale's answer sounded familiar to me. I'd heard it before, and it sounded just as great as ever.

"Because Michael will win in my car."

CHAPTER 17

TESTING, TESTING

It was a pretty but cold Tuesday morning in Sherrills Ford when the alarm went off at six. I kissed Buffy on the forehead and told her I was off to test with my new racing team. I knew the path to victory for me—winning in NASCAR's top division—ran straight through Rockingham, North Carolina. If I was going to have success in 2001, I'd have to win my team over in Rockingham.

The short-long wait for NAPA, my show-me-where-to-sign negotiations with Dale, the press conference announcing to the world that I'd be joining one of the best teams in NASCAR—all that was accomplished now. Laying down laps on the track was what I was facing next.

I had to prove to my new team I was that guy, the guy who could take us all to Victory Lane.

The NASCAR season starts every year with the Super Bowl, the big one, the Daytona 500. But when the checkered flag falls at Daytona, we have only five days to be in Rockingham, North Carolina, ready for race number two. You see, while some races are more prestigious than others, they all pay the same number of points. And to be the NASCAR champion, you need the most points. So in the grand scheme of things, that makes Rockingham or any other race just as important as Daytona.

They call the track in Rockingham "the Rock." It is located just a couple of hours down the road from Charlotte, the epicenter of NASCAR. All the top Cup teams turn up each January in Rockingham to test their new cars. I knew this was an especially important test for me. This was my first test with my new team. The majority of the races are on tracks like Rockingham. Daytona and Talladega, they are different animals. It takes a different kind of car and a different kind of driving to be successful at those places. And despite my overall crappy record, no one ever questioned my Daytona prowess. I always got props there and at Talladega, the two resistor-plate tracks. It was most all the other places we raced like the Rock where people questioned my skills.

This was a real getting-to-know-each-other period for me and my team—and me getting to know my new car as well. One thing I wanted them to know about me was that I could win anywhere.

One thing was for sure: One way or the other, good or bad, first impressions were going to be made.

I had circled the Rockingham test on the calendar the day I signed to drive for Dale. I knew a good test at Rockingham would be a sign that we could run well anywhere. I needed a good test. I had to get my new team to buy into me being their driver. It takes a team to win in NASCAR, everyone believing in each other. A good test would be a good start toward that.

I was coming off a couple pretty tough years in NASCAR Cup competition. Two top fives in two years was all I had to hang my hat on. I'm sure everyone at DEI knew that, as well as they knew that by the end of the 2000 season I had pushed my losing streak to 462. That's right: 0–462. My goal during the off-season was to win my new team over. As long as I was smart and drove hard, I believed they would overlook my record because Dale had.

As I drove toward the Rock, I put together in my head what my goals were for this first test day with my new team. I had raced for Dale at Rockingham twice before in his Busch Series car. I finished second there in 1994, nearly taking the win late from Mark Martin. That was that time Dale called me the P-word. There was a late caution that day, and I jumped on the radio to the crew and said: "Give me two tires and a bottle of water." I was running second and was confident I could win with my strategy.

"We're taking four tires and you don't have time for water, your P-word," Dale shouted back. "Just shut up and drive."

I'm not a camel, I thought. And I'm not a P-word either. But I muttered to myself: "I hear you, Big E. I'll just shut up and drive."

I laugh every time I think about Dale saying that. But in the upcoming two-day test, there was a different P-word that would be key to success.

Patience.

I wanted to be fast, of course. But we were not going to Rockingham to set a track record. My crew chief, Scott Eggleston, had told me we were just going there to gather information. "Collect data," I believe was the phrase he used. And DEI had a fancy way of collecting data I had never used before. Telemetry. When I got out on the track, this telemetry would shoot real-time information back to the crews in the pit area. They could see what I was doing while I was doing it. The cars would be analyzed very closely, and I knew I would be too. I'd never had a car that could tell on me before. I knew it would be important that day for my impressions from the seat to match up with what the engineers were seeing on their computer screens. I'd always been envious of other drivers whose teams used this fancy testing equipment. Now it was making me nervous.

When I'd about made it to Rockingham, I decided to call Dale. He answered the phone with: "You there yet?"

"I'm near," I said. "You got any advice?"

Dale's message mainly related to what I had said earlier. It related to patience: "Don't overdrive your car. Don't push it too hard. Just try to feel your car." I knew all that. Every race-car driver knows that. Sounded like a bunch of clichés to me. I guess I was hoping he was going to wave some magic wand over me that would make me faster than I'd ever been before. But I knew better than that. There's no magic in racing. It's pretty black-and-white. It's whoever can get their car to handle better than the next guy. And when it's time to go at the end of the race, go hard.

So my job mainly was just to log some laps in my #15 NAPA Chevy so my crew could collect their data. And that's what I did. For eight hours. Lap after lap. And while I tried to be patient in getting them their data, it was difficult. All that repetition was driving me nuts.

Computers don't lie. And although I didn't know a huge amount about all the data we were collecting, the data that was most important to me was on the top left corner of the screen, and that was lap time. And Steve Park's was way better than mine. So was Dale Junior's.

These damn teammates that I wanted so badly, and this telemetry that I was so envious of—they were making this day a real pain. The ride back from Rockingham that evening felt twice as long as the one down. To make it worse, Dale called.

"How'd it go?" he asked.

I wondered if that was a question he knew the answer to or genuinely was wondering.

"Not good," I told him. "Junior and Park were both fast. A couple of tenths a lap faster than me."

"What did I tell you this morning?" he shot back, a question I didn't think I was supposed to answer.

"Patience," he said. "This is your first day on the track with your new team. Take your time. Get to know your guys. Tonight, all three teams will get together and come up with a plan for tomorrow. That's what teammates are for."

I was an old dog who needed to learn some new tricks. How in the world would I know what teammates were for? I'd never had any of those. But I had them now. And I needed to learn how to use them.

Something I decided on my own, however, was I didn't much like logging laps just so they could collect their stupid data. I wanted to change some stuff. And we didn't change much of anything all day.

That was one thing I did enjoy about my old crew chief, Bobby Kennedy. We didn't have any data-collecting devices. He just looked at me and said: "What do you want to try?" And I looked at him and said the same.

That was the way I used to do things. But that was the old dog. The new one needed to be patient. Old Dog was about to get New Dog in trouble by being too pushy. But Old Dog's record sucked.

So I just did what Dale told me to do at Rockingham back in 1994. I just shut up and drove.

When I returned for day two of the test, the same data-collecting continued. About halfway through the day, the engineers told me they had all the data they needed and asked me if there were any changes I wanted to try.

Finally! My patience had paid off. There were a couple of spring changes that had helped at Rockingham before, and I wanted to try them again. They could collect some data on that.

I wanted to give some input and see if it helped the car's performance. I felt like it would. And I didn't want to leave this important getting-to-know-each-other session without giving my crew some idea of how I wanted the car to feel.

Was I ever glad I did!

Two front spring changes and a sway bar later and—*boom*! The lap times were just as fast as my teammates'. And just as consistent. It made sense to me. A car's a car. Dale's cars probably had the best engines I'd ever had. And the aerodynamics were way more refined than anything I'd ever driven as well.

So if you have a good motor and you have a good car and the driver knows what he's doing, the lap time should show it and all that telemetry can ride right along.

And those engineers with their college degrees looking at their squiggly lines, I don't care if they take credit for it. I just want to be fast.

Now, as the test was ending, I was just that.

Fast.

The ride home that day was a whole lot cheerier than the one the day before. The day before, I didn't want to answer when Dale was calling. And now I couldn't wait to call him.

His little project had stepped up and run some fast laps for him. Then again, isn't that why he hired me?

CHAPTER 18

DAYTONA BOUND

I'd done my share of losing over the past fifteen years—and maybe a couple of other people's share too. But I didn't feel like a loser anymore.

I didn't care what the record book said. I didn't care what condescending questions the reporters might ask. The Michael Waltrip who was on his way to Daytona in 2001 under Dale Earnhardt's wing? This Michael was undefeated, and he was walking around acting like it. This Michael knew he could win. And back at the factory in Mooresville, the team knew it too.

During the winter, I had done my job. I had won my team over. They believed in me now. None of them seemed the least bit concerned about my stupid record, and neither was I. We were just race-car people, heading for the first and biggest race of the year. Man, I felt like a kid again, like that kid back in Kentucky who used to sit at his desk at Stanley Elementary School just waiting for his parents to scoop him up and deliver him to NASCAR's holy land.

Most years at Daytona, the pre-race routine was pretty much the same.

You had to get your picture taken in your new uniform. I stood there proudly in my NAPA blue. You had to do interviews about the upcoming season. I did one after another. It seemed like everyone wanted to ask about me driving for Dale.

Why not? This year, my story was better than most. I was the guy who'd never won, driving for the guy whose name meant winning. It was a solid two days of media swirl.

What an unlikely pair we were! Just like we'd always been: the Intimidator and the Intimidated. No one could question Dale's record. Everyone had questioned mine.

Back in my little world in Sherrills Ford, I was the guy in charge. People looked to me for direction. Put me with Dale though: He was Batman and I was Robin. Holy skid marks, Dale! Whatever you say!

Over the years, wherever we were, people would look at us and think: What do those two have in common? If we were on the boat, it was "Why's the guy in the funny sunglasses and the mustache hanging around with the dude in the loud pink shorts?" In New York City, "Why's the champ having dinner with the seventeenth-place guy?" It didn't matter where we were, people didn't get it. Now here we were in Daytona, and suddenly, to me at least, we didn't seem that different at all. This was serious business here. We'd come with one thing in mind: taking the Daytona 500 trophy back home to North Carolina with us.

I wanted everyone to see us as one. Owner and driver, one and the same, working together for a common goal. We were there to win. As we prepared for the race, I could tell that this was Dale's mind-set as well. I wasn't "goofy Mike" in Daytona, like I could be when we were on the boat. I was his driver. He had been working with me for months, making sure I was mentally prepared to win.

Dale was cool. I guess he thought he was being subtle. But I got it. I'd heard his interviews. He'd say, "You better watch that #15 car. You better watch Michael. Keep your eyes on Michael. He's the sleeper in Daytona this year."

He was using the pre-Daytona media to send messages to me. Messages I was getting. I didn't 100-percent-for-sure know at the time where these messages were coming from. Looking back now it was as plain as the mask on Batman's face. Dale's plan was to make sure I knew what he expected from me. And that was a win.

I know now he was just saying it to make sure I heard it. Gotcha, boss! Loud and clear!

Everything up until practice began on Friday was just hype, spreading the story of Dale's new driver. We were delivering our story to the media and the fans. That's what this period was for. There were no cars on the track yet. NASCAR needed us to be doing something to make sure all the tickets got sold.

"Say something even if you make it up," they were probably thinking. But we weren't making anything up at all. We were there with one goal in mind.

Everyone's dream of winning the race seemed downright plausible, even the championship. Before this race began, everyone was tied for the lead in points. Even a winless driver with a new team had no fewer points than a seven-time champion did.

Las Vegas had set my odds of winning the 500 at 40 to 1. Most would say that was optimistic. They probably should have been more like 462 to 1. Maybe more. My goal was to make the 462 joke irrelevant.

Daddy used to say, "Money talks, and bullshit walks." I'm not sure how that applies here. But as practice was getting ready to begin, it seemed to relate. All the P.R. B.S. was fixing to take a backseat to what mattered the most: cars on the track. Whaddaya got? What can you do? How fast can you go? It was time to "put up or shut up." That was something else Dad said. And that definitely applied today.

The first practice session of the year at Daytona was always the most anticipated. Not just because it was the first practice, but because it was Daytona. Winning at Daytona can define your career. And when practice starts, if you've got a fast car, that means you have a shot. In my case, with a new team, we couldn't afford to waste a lot of time trying to catch up. We needed to be up front right from the beginning.

When I rolled onto the track for the first official practice session with my new #15 car and my new team, we were plenty fast. Very competitive.

As I made my way through the days and nights at Daytona, I was feeling quite comfortable. In qualifying that was held the week before, our NAPA team posted a solid time. We were top fifteen, earning us a solid start in our qualifying race that Thursday. My car was very fast, and I was very ready.

You know how much I've always loved the qualifying races at Daytona.

Now here we were, twenty-five years later. I didn't wake up in a hotel that morning after driving all night from Kentucky in a smoke-filled Chevy. When I woke up I was through that tunnel, in the infield, in my bus.

I had all the enthusiasm I'd had when I was that twelve-year-old boy though. Today was going to be my day. I wanted to deliver a statement to the whole NASCAR world: Anyone who wanted to win the Daytona 500 on Sunday would have to beat me to do it. I wanted there to be no doubt about that.

I was going to make that point loud and clear in my qualifying race. And that was just a couple of hours away.

CHAPTER 19

DALE'S PLAN

I t was time to strap myself in for my first race of the 2001 NASCAR season, the twin 125-mile qualifiers for the Daytona 500.

These twins would set the field for Sunday's running of the Great American Race. This was the first opportunity for my team and me to show our owner and the whole NASCAR world that we were here and we were going to contend. Confidence was no problem at all. Dale had been getting me ready for this day since he hired me in 2000—actually even before that, with his you'd-win-in-my-car speeches. He believed I could win. He believed in me. He had gotten me to the point where I believed it too.

And then there was the late restart. I had positioned myself perfectly to win that day and make a statement. I wanted to show the competition that I and my team had what it took to win in Daytona. Instead of delivering that statement, I made a mistake behind the wheel that cost me the race.

Eager to show everyone I was there to win, I messed up. I just simply missed a shift. I didn't shift cleanly from second to third gear and lost my momentum. When the momentum was lost, so was the race.

I had it all set up. I could see exactly what I needed to do to win my qualifying race, but I didn't execute. And I was right. What I saw would have won me that race. However, my missed shift caused me to finish eighth or ninth.

That night, my mistake ate at me. No wonder you've never won a race, I thought. You can't even shift gears. All the work Dale had done to prepare me mentally to win the 500 was in jeopardy.

He had gotten me into such a great place. Now I was confused. I didn't think I had what it took to win, not after what I had just done. That's where I was mentally, not exactly the frame of mind you want to take into any race, much less the Daytona 500.

I was really beating myself up over what had happened. That night, I tried to explain it all to Buffy. As any wife would, she tried to comfort me. "That's just part of it," she said. "Get over it. You'll do great on Sunday. Just remember: You put yourself in a position to win today. You can do it again Sunday."

I certainly appreciated her effort, but I can't say it did me much good. When I went to bed that night, my head was filled with doubt.

At Daytona, the motor-home area where the drivers stay is adjacent to the garage where the race cars are parked. The drivers' and owners' coaches are located in this area during race week. We're all running back and forth to the garage area, hosting meet-and-greets with our sponsors, trading stories and gossip with each other, and, sometimes, making predictions about the race.

My motor home was parked near Jeff Gordon's and Sterling Marlin's, and Dale Earnhardt's was off to the left. Thursday night's sleep was not very therapeutic. When I got up Friday morning, I did my best to file away in my mind what had happened the day before. But it still had me a little messed up. As I walked by Dale's motor home, I heard a sharp "Hey!"

It was Dale's unmistakable bark.

I looked over and saw a small opening in the front door. Dale's head was sticking out.

"Get over here," he said.

That's just how Dale was. Short, direct, and very much to the point. Sometimes, even if he was in a great mood, that's what you'd get. Blunt sentences, never any doubt about what he was trying to say. And now I, his brand-new driver and longtime friend, who didn't know how to shift gears, was fixing to get an earful, I was sure.

Man, I thought, I bet he's gonna cuss me. He's gonna cuss me out for screwin' up that restart yesterday when I should have won that race.

And he'd be right. That's exactly what I'd done. There was no excuse. I ain't twelve, I thought. I'm thirty-seven. I can shift a gear, right? Do your job and you win. Oh, me! This is gonna be painful.

Dale never yelled at me. Except for that one day in Rockingham when he called me the P-word. That was actually funny, but this wasn't going to be. I wasn't sure how Dale would handle the mistake I made. As I approached him and thought about it, I had no idea what I would get.

"Where you goin'?" he asked through the door of his bus as I walked up.

"To the garage area to check on the boys," I told him.

Dale glared at me, then motioned for me to come inside. I was uncomfortable. When I entered the bus, it was just Ty and Dale sitting there. Dale surprised me again. Instead of asking what the hell happened, his demeanor instantly lightened up. He said in an enthusiastic tone: "We're gonna win this race Sunday."

Okay, I thought. Excuse me? What did he just say? How could he say that after what I did yesterday? Was he not paying attention?

"Damn, Dale," I said. "I shoulda won that race."

"What?" he said. "I shoulda won that race. Not you. I didn't win it either. Listen. That don't matter. Yesterday's yesterday. Forget about that. Pay attention to me. I'm gonna tell you how we're gonna win this race Sunday. With the rules the way they are this year, it's a different animal. It's gonna be wide open out there."

There, right there, another Dale lesson was being taught. All week long—heck, for months—he'd been preparing me for this race. And now here we were on Friday morning, talking for the first time after my screwup the day before, and he didn't seem to care about it in the least.

He was past that. Worrying about not winning on Thursday wasn't going to help us now.

"We're gonna win Sunday," he said. "That's what we're here for, and that's what we're gonna do."

Dale clearly had something in mind. Why hadn't he mentioned it before? I don't know. But he was telling me about it now.

"You can't win here alone anymore," he said. "It ain't like it used to be. We gotta work together—me, you, and Dale Junior." He repeated the last phrase. "Me, you, and Dale Junior. Together we're gonna win the race."

We had a fourth driver on the team, Steve Park. So I said, "Yeah, and Park can help, too, right?"

If three working together was good, four had to be better.

I guess not.

Dale shook his head. "Nah, I wouldn't count on that," he said. "He don't understand the draft as well as we do. I wouldn't count on him being around."

Well, shoot, I thought to myself. Park's pretty good. He won DEI's first Cup race at Watkins Glen. But that wasn't what I said. What I said was, "Okay. Cool. How exactly are we gonna do this?"

"We're gonna work together—it's that simple," Dale said. "Whichever of us gets to the front, at the end we're gonna push and we're gonna make sure that person stays in the front. That's the only way to win at Daytona with the rules we got. It'll be the three of us against all of them at the end."

I liked the way that sounded. Dale went on. "I won at Talladega, going from eighteenth to the lead in two laps," he said. "And the reason why is 'cause Kenny Wallace got hooked to my back bumper and he didn't let me go. We just went together. Herman was dedicated to me and that's why I won that race."

"And Herm got second," I said.

(We called Kenny Wallace "Herman." I don't know exactly why. In NASCAR, it seems most everybody has a nickname. Dale had three or four. For some reason, I don't have any.)

"This time," Dale said, "you, me, and Dale Junior—we're gonna be dedicated to each other, and that's how we're gonna do it."

That sounded like a good idea to me. That finish at Talladega was amazing. He raced from the middle of the pack to the win in just two laps. No one had ever done that before. Then again, no one had ever done a lot of things that Dale had done.

I guess the way Dale had won Talladega and what he'd seen in the qualifiers on Thursday had him thinking about what we needed to do Sunday. He had a plan and wanted to make sure I understood it.

All this talk was new to me. I may have looked a bit confused because Dale threw a Sharpie at me and said: "You understand what I'm sayin', right?"

Ouch! Right between the eyes!

He repeated: "We will get together at the front. And when we do, we're staying there. Locked together."

"Yes, sir, boss, I get it loud and clear. You can count on me."

I had never had teammates in a race before. I was liking how this felt. We had a plan. That makes sense, right? If you go into a battle, you'd better have a plan. The Daytona 500 has always been a battle. And in 2001, it was set to be the most competitive, toughest fight in the history of the 500.

Dale had it all figured out, and I was down with the plan. Dale spoke confidently, making sure he drilled the message into my head.

One question I did have, however, was Dale Junior.

"Did you tell Dale Junior the plan?" I asked.

"Don't worry about Dale Junior," Dale said. "I'll tell him. He'll do what I say. We just have to survive early. Do whatever you need to do to make sure you're around at the end. Whoever gets to the front first stays there."

Dale spoke confidently, making sure he'd drilled the message into my head. He had.

This was less than twenty-four hours after my screwup. I'd spent the night wanting to slit my own throat. I hated not having performed like I should have, like Dale expected me to. But all of a sudden, it was Friday morning and Dale was saying what he said—and I was back in business.

I walked off that bus and said, "Woo-hoo! Heck, yeah!"

Just minutes after that, as I thought about that meeting in Dale's bus, I was sure I'd never had anybody talk to me like that before. Heck, I'd never had a teammate. Now I had a whole team. And I'd had an owner lay out a real plan. And that owner was Dale Earnhardt.

Forgive me if it took Dale yelling at me to understand what he was saying. But, look, this whole idea, this strategy of working together with the other drivers and being committed to one another—that wasn't only new to me, it was new to NASCAR. I had never looked in my mirror for one second and thought that the driver behind me was there to help me. I'm pretty sure no other driver ever had either.

I always thought the other guy was there to take my spot away and shuffle me out.

But if the three of us could be there at the end—well, maybe not. We would be in it together.

Dale's strategy was for us to work together. As Dale explained it, we were going to team up in order to make sure we put our cars at the front of the pack. This is just a different way of thinking about racing. My job had always been to block the guy behind me. He's got all this extra power because I'm busting the air in front of him.

If I don't block him, he's going to pass me. That's what we do. That's how you race. Or at least that's how we always had. But like Talladega in 2000, the rules for the 2001 Daytona 500 were extremely different. The action would be intense. The only flaw in Dale's plan, as I saw it, was how hard it would be for the three of us to race to the front of forty other cars at the end. I loved the plan, but it seemed a little unrealistic.

That was obvious to me even as I was sitting in Dale's motor home getting his idea into my head. "Down to the end" is a long way away from lap one. There's a lot of stuff that's going to go on. If we were going to be able to work together at the end, we would first have to make it through the start.

There are forty other cars out there. There are two hundred laps. We would be all over that track—blown engines, wrecks, a lot of stuff would happen. But you know, nothing in my conversation with Dale that morning made me think he doubted we'd get the chance to execute his plan.

And who was I to doubt Dale Earnhardt?

I couldn't wait for Sunday.

CHAPTER 20

RACE DAY

Race mornings are more relaxing than you might think, even the morning of the biggest race of the year.

Sure, there's pressure. You always remember what you're there for: to drive a car faster than a whole bunch of other guys who are really good at driving their cars fast.

Sounds very simple, right? Well, if you think that's easy, you've never tried it on a Sunday afternoon in a NASCAR Cup Series race. These boys are good. There's nothing easy about it.

All the NASCAR drivers are really talented. Everyone shows up with fast cars. To win, not only do you have to be fast, you also have to survive. One small mistake can mean instant disaster. And as you get yourself mentally and physically prepared, you have to have a checklist of a million little and not-so-little details.

1. *Am I properly hydrated? Check.*
2. *Did I get plenty of sleep? Check.*
3. *Did I remember to go to the bathroom? Check.*
4. *How's my mental health? Hmm, let me get back to you on that one.*

To be a serious NASCAR racer you need a combination of brains and balls, an ability to analyze a dangerous situation and conveniently overlook the danger part. You have to be slightly crazy to win at

Daytona. But if you're too crazy, you'll crash, and you can't win if you crash.

It was race morning at the Daytona 500. The usual race-day pressures were magnified because this was Daytona, and even more so for me personally. The 2001 Daytona was my first race driving for Dale Earnhardt, Inc.—DEI. The Man. Dale Earnhardt.

Everything else was the same as usual. At the drop of the green flag, we would be doing basically the same things: Pass cars. Miss wrecks. And try to win. These were my goals, goals I'd had in every race for the last fifteen years. But in 462 starts, the winning part had eluded me.

This race day, February 18, 2001, began for me like most race mornings did: with my wife and daughter in our motor home at the track, in this case the legendary Daytona International Speedway—and some nice, relaxing family time. That's how we do it in NASCAR. Prepare like crazy, race like hell. But before and after, spend some quality time with the family.

The three of us—Buffy, Macy, and I—were extremely comfortable in our motor home. It was pretty nice, a Newell with everything you could possibly need—a living room, a bedroom, a bathroom, a kitchen, dishes, food, a TV, a computer, stuff to read, all your basic appliances, all within easy reach.

I loved the fact that everything was just right there. The bed was certainly comfortable. I got a good night's sleep. That's always crucial. You don't want to be sleep-deprived at 190 miles an hour. You need every possible ounce of energy.

Early that morning, Buffy was up making breakfast for Macy. I was still lying in bed, half asleep. That wasn't unusual—for me or for Buffy. What happened next wasn't unusual either. While I lay in bed, Macy came running into the room and started jumping on my head. She landed right on me and said, "Let's wassle, Dad!"

I loved it. She was three, so cute and full of herself. She didn't care if this was race day at Daytona. She just wanted to play. She thought it was pretty funny to sneak up on her daddy while he was still half asleep and start jumping up and down on his head.

Although I knew it was coming, I always acted surprised.

"Macy!" I said. "Where did you come from?"

"It's time, Daddy," she said, giggling and looking totally proud of herself. "Mom said you need to get up."

I grabbed her and said: "Mom said? Or Macy said?"—as I got her in position to become a victim of the great wassler himself, the Tickle Monster.

"Mom said!" I tickled her legs and asked her again: "Who said?"

This time I got the correct answer. "Macy said," she answered as she laughed wildly.

That had become a morning ritual of ours. Although I didn't really like getting up, that was the best way of doing so: my beautiful little girl in my arms and the smell of breakfast cooking in the kitchen about four feet away.

That's how it went on this particular race morning, the equivalent of waking up anywhere on the NASCAR circuit with my family. This morning, we just happened to be in the motor home in the infield at Daytona on the biggest day of the year. We were camped out in a long line of other motor homes with race-car drivers and their families. Plus a couple hundred thousand people wandering around, ready for the Daytona experience. But as the day began, I wasn't a race-car driver. I was just Daddy. And being Daddy was the greatest feeling in the whole world.

My niece, Dana Carol, was our nanny. Her mom and dad are my sister Connie and her husband, David. Connie and David both worked for us back in North Carolina. Like Mom, they were also our neighbors. Dana's job was to help with Macy and make sure she was ready for the day. She arrived just as the wasslin' match was breaking up. I pulled myself out of bed, got showered, and came out to the living room. The crowd in the bus continued to grow. Daughter Caitlin and her little sister were now there.

As I made it to the living room and looked out to see the activity that was building at the track, I really began to think about the racing part of my day. I thought about how special Daytona was to me, how well I had always performed there. But at Daytona, you're never really certain how well your day will go. Still, I was certain this day had the potential of being very, very special.

I knew the NAPA car, Dale's car, the car I'd be driving, could win the Daytona 500.

I knew it. And the time to do it was coming.

But I needed to remain calm and put any negative thoughts out of my head. Forget Thursday.

"Don't worry about your record," I told myself. "This is race one driving for Dale, not race 463 in an extension of a record of disappointment."

I was having many conversations with myself: "You can win it. . . . Be calm. . . . Stay focused." I wasn't much into being sociable. I was just sort of zoning out. I was semi-engaged, I guess.

We had breakfast. I got dressed. The TV was on. There were people running around everywhere. I played with Macy on the floor for a little bit. She brought out her Barbie dolls. Buffy was cleaning up the kitchen. But even though the race didn't start until one P.M., my brain had already begun to shift. Buffy recognized that mentally I was somewhere else, and she respected that.

I was still in the motor-home living room, still physically there. But I couldn't stop thinking about the race. "You've got the car, and we've got the plan." Then I argued with myself. "But will the plan work? Quit questioning Dale's plan. He's the Man. Just be cool and calm and make sure you're there at the end. That's your job. That's what Dale said. Get to the end."

I was thinking about all those things that morning and gradually growing more and more distant from everyone because of the significance of the day.

Finally, it was time to head out for the race-morning hospitality visits. But this year, because I was driving for Dale, I had more sponsors than ever. Hospitality for Coca-Cola, hospitality for Oreos, hospitality for NAPA, hospitality here, hospitality there. After signing about a thousand autographs and telling all my new sponsors how I was going to win the race for them that day, it was time to head to the drivers' meeting.

NASCAR requires all the drivers and crew chiefs to attend these meetings before every race. But at Daytona, the meeting was an event. Hundreds of people packed into a small room to see and be seen. The actual meetings themselves were generally pretty routine, pretty boring. We were told just about the same thing every week, like "When the caution comes out, slow down." Duh! "Be careful on Pit Road." "Don't jump the restarts." "Listen to your spotters."

*Above: **FUTURE RACER:**
How 'bout that hair and
snazzy silk shirt on a
twelve-year-old?*
Courtesy of the Waltrip Family

*Right: **MOMMA'S BOY:**
With my mom, Marga-
ret Jean Evans Waltrip,
at home in Owensboro,
Kentucky.*
Courtesy of the Waltrip Family

Above: LUNCH WITH ROYALTY:
Me with King Richard, wife Lynda, and son Kyle Petty. Eating out of the back of a van.
RacingOne/ISC Archives/ Getty Images

Left: PROUD PARENTS:
Celebrating Mother's Day with Leroy and Margaret.
Courtesy of the Waltrip Family

Left: BAHAMA BOYS:
Me and Dale with Captain Terry (right) and mate after a good day fishing.
Courtesy of the Waltrip Family

Right: BIG E:
The seven-time champion defined NASCAR and made me a winner.
Jamie Squire/Getty Images Sport/Getty Images

Opposite Page: BIG WIN:
Buffy and me after the All-Star race, my first official victory—well, not really.
Dozier Mobley/Getty Images Sport/Getty Images

Above: GOLFING BUDDIES:
*Enjoying a beautiful day
with my dad.*
Courtesy of the Waltrip Family

Right: ONE TO GO:
*Just like Dale said it would
be. Me, Dale Junior, and
Dale, racing toward the
perfect finish. We thought.*
**Bill Frakes/Sports Illustrated/
Getty Images**

**Opposite Page:
VICTORY LANE:**
*After the Daytona 500,
before I knew.*
**Jamie Squire/Getty Images Sport/
Getty Images**

Above: *UNBELIEVABLE LOSS:*
A week later in Rockingham, trying to make sense of it all.
Donald Miralle/Getty Images Sport/Getty Images

WINDING DOWN:
With Macy at the last
race of my last full
season, Miami 2009.
Still have the hair!
Autostock

Above: BEHIND THE WHEEL:
Strapped in and ready to go.
Jason Smith/Getty Images Sport/Getty Images

ALL THE KIDS: *Mom with Bobby,*
Connie, Carolyn, Darrell, and Mike
Courtesy of the Waltrip Family

Spotters, they're interesting folks—the driver's eye in the sky. For safety purposes, they're required by NASCAR. Spotters are positioned high atop the grandstand so they can see the whole track. If someone spins out, your spotter tells you that the caution's out and where the trouble is and to slow down. That is why they are there. But over time, the spotters started doing more than just warning you about problems. They began assisting the drivers. "Clean high," your spotter will say. "Three wide . . . you got one looking low." Spotters make sure the driver is fully aware of what is going on around him.

I don't really like spotters. It's nothing personal. I just don't like what they do. I think drivers should drive and the spotters should do what they were originally put up there for—to warn drivers about track conditions. But actually, at places like Daytona and Talladega, they are pretty helpful, I guess. We run so close together, we need all the information we can get to keep us from making a mistake that could cause a huge pileup.

My spotter was Chuck Joyce. Chuckie was pretty cool. He had spotted for me when I drove for Wood Brothers and had done a good job. So when I went to DEI, I asked him to come along. I loved Chuckie. He was fun. He was a travel agent. He didn't know squat about racing. But he could see and speak, and he had a pulse. So he was qualified to be a spotter.

Before NASCAR gets into all the race procedure stuff, they introduce the celebrities, dignitaries, and sponsor folks who are in attendance. On this day, NASCAR welcomed our new broadcast partner to the sport. Fox and NBC had committed to cover all the NASCAR races. All through the eighties and nineties, our fan base had kept growing and growing. Fox and NBC wanted to be part of the action. This was a big deal for NASCAR. All our events would be on network TV—and just two networks. Prior to the 2001 season, our races were all over the TV. CBS had a few. ESPN had some. TNT, TBS. Seemed like most everybody but the Playboy channel and SOAPnet had a race.

This was significant for NASCAR. Fox and NBC paid a premium for the broadcast rights. It was also significant for my brother Darrell. He had retired from driving at the end of the 2000 season and was quickly signed by Fox to be part of their race-day coverage team. All the Fox broadcasters including Darrell were introduced at the meeting and were set to call all the action of the forty-third running of the Daytona 500. I was making my first start for Dale. Darrell was going to be calling his first race for Fox. Wouldn't this be a great day for another first—my first win?

When the meeting ended, I headed off toward my bus to find a quick bite to eat, get my uniform on, and prepare myself to race. That had always been the routine for me. But on the way to the bus lot, I decided to change directions. I needed some quiet time. I was sure my motor home, full of family members and friends, would be far from quiet.

Instead I walked toward the race-car hauler. The hauler is a fifty-three-foot tractor-trailer that serves as the team's headquarters during race weekends. Like the cars, the haulers are all parked tightly in line, side by side, and lined up by points. At Daytona, the haulers are parked in order according to the way they finished in points the previous year.

The guy who's first in points gets the best spot—then second, third, and all the way down through the field. When you got to the end, that's where we sat. We were a brand-new team. We had zero points. So my truck was way down there with nobody around it.

When I got to it, instead of going inside, I walked around and sat down on the front bumper. I stayed there by myself for ten or fifteen minutes and thought. This was a special time for me, fifteen minutes in deep, personal thought. That short time of reflection was crucial to my winning the Daytona 500, and it happened an hour before the race. I don't think I could have performed like I did if I hadn't had that time to myself.

I was thinking: It's here. It's time to race the Daytona 500, the most important race of your career, Mike. You can win in this car. You know that. Today, we're gonna make sure to be there at the end and let everyone know it.

I knew it was important not to let all the excitement and enthusiasm force me into doing something stupid. "You can't win this thing at the start," I told myself. "The race is five hundred miles long. So take it easy. No mistakes. Focus."

I thought about Dale's plan, my car, the competition, and everything I needed to consider to win. And with that, I got up and walked off.

I think this impromptu meeting I called with myself was an extension of the coaching Dale had been giving me since September. He was rubbing off on me, and that was a good thing. I had certainly put the negative thoughts of Thursday behind me. I had turned it around. I remembered Buffy's words: "You put yourself in a position to win that race on Thursday. You can do it Sunday too. Now go do it. Just make sure you finish the deal this time."

I had seen myself make mistakes before in my career. Maybe I had a car I thought I could win with, and I just pushed too hard.

Obviously, I must have been doing something wrong along the way. I had to be different today. Dale had me confident I would be. Sitting on the bumper of the truck in the middle of this whirlwind of action and the hustle-bustle of people everywhere, I'd slipped away and found a moment where I could just focus on what it was going to take to win. Focus on being patient for the first part of this race in order to be able to make sure I was around at the end, along with Dale and Dale Junior.

Certainly, there was no guarantee I'd be there at the end, no matter where I was mentally. But trusting my skills and being calm would give me the best chance.

I found a quiet, tranquil moment of clarity in the middle of thousands of people. I had blocked all those people out. It was just me and my thoughts on the bumper of a big, ol' truck.

That was important. Afterward I went back to the motor home. I was right: That place wasn't quiet at all. In fact, it was quite hectic. I grabbed a quick bite to eat, put on my uniform, hugged everyone, and cleared that chaos.

It was time for Buffy and me to head toward Pit Road. It's about a quarter-mile from where the buses are to where the cars are parked on Pit Road. The teams spend Sunday morning going through checklists of a hundred things on the cars, making sure the suspension is tight, the brakes are bled, etc., etc. They have just an endless number of items to check. One of the crew members has a responsibility for ten things, another crew member for another ten things. So they spend all Sunday morning making the final preparations and adjustments to the cars. Then they go through inspection—NASCAR inspection. When they're out of inspection and they pass, they go sit on Pit Road in the order in which they're gonna start the race.

By the time noon rolled around, we were on our way to Pit Road.

All the cars were there. The drivers were all making their way out for pre-race activities including getting introduced, meeting the dignitaries, and waving at the fans. I was in my uniform. Buffy had on a blue pantsuit with a light-blue leather coat. She always dressed up nicely for the races. She looked beautiful.

We met up with Dale and Teresa. Buffy had asked Teresa when she and Dale were going to walk out because we wanted to walk with them. Along the way, we were laughing; I was enjoying a walk with my friend, my car owner and our wives, getting ready for my first race for the man who had given me this wonderful opportunity, and, in general, just being really relaxed and enjoying this experience.

We were signing the occasional autograph on the way for fans who asked and just reminiscing or talking about life in general. Not really talking any race strategy at this point. I knew what I was supposed to do. We had covered that on Friday. Now it was just a matter of getting ready to start the race.

I had gone through all kinds of stuff in my brain. What Dale and I talked about. Adjustments me and my crew chief, Scott, had tried during the qualifying races and practice—which ones were good and which ones were bad. Now it was: Just go execute. Go do it.

Walking out with Dale made me feel different. I was so happy with where I was mentally. This time out, I knew in my brain—I didn't just think it, I knew it—I could win this race. My car was perfect in final practice Saturday afternoon. Not only was it fast, it handled great. Handling is very important at Daytona. I was confident about my car. That's one thing that was different. I'd never, ever had a car this good. It had it all.

I was also thinking about the meeting we'd had on Friday morning after Thursday's qualifying races, where Dale had mapped out how we were going to win this race. That meeting was amazing to me. How did he figure it all out? I don't think anyone else had. I know one guy who didn't.

It was the first meeting I'd ever had like that. I can't imagine anyone had ever had a meeting like that. Dale told me how we were going to do it. Dale knew more about winning at Daytona than anyone. He had won more races there than anyone. Man, I loved my leader! Racing for

Dale was going to be so cool, I thought. He had me right where I needed to be. 0-fer-whatever? I couldn't care less about that anymore.

It'll be me, Dale, and Dale Junior.

I figured Dale must have talked to Dale Junior, right? I hoped Junior was down with that plan.

CHAPTER 21

GREEN FLAG

U ntil lap fifty or so, I just ran in the pack. I didn't make many moves. I didn't take any chances. I just hung on. That was my plan early in the going that day. I didn't have anything to gain by pushing too hard too soon. There have been times when I gave myself good direction then didn't follow it. This time, I actually took my own advice. I'm happy about that.

My car wasn't handling exactly like I wanted. It was loose. If you're a race person, you know what I mean by that. And if you're not, it's funny that you're reading my book. Anyway, when I would go into the turns, the car just wouldn't handle like I wanted. The rear end was wanting to swing around. And when you're running 200 miles an hour, side by side, sometimes three wide, that's not good. I was telling my crew chief over the radio, "It's just not right. I can't get the back end under me." That just about describes it: Every time I'd try to make a move and I got in a tight squeeze, it would want to spin out. So my pre-race game plan was key: My car wasn't ready to charge, and I'd convinced myself I shouldn't be charging that early anyway.

So I was managing an ill-handling car, along with not being overly in a hurry. I was just trying to log laps until I could get in the pit and have my crew make some adjustments.

"It's loose—not terrible loose but sorta loose," I told the crew before the first stop. "I'd say a six loose on a scale of one to ten. We need to work on it. I'd say a little wedge, but I'll leave it up to y'all."

After we pitted, I was pleased. The adjustments we made addressed my problem perfectly. In just one pit stop, the crew nailed it. That's unusual for a new crew. There are about a dozen things they could have done to it based on my feedback, and they picked the right ones.

Now that the car was right, I needed to see what I had. It was time to get going and see what I could do. I needed to know how much car I had under me. I didn't want to wait any longer. Fifty laps, sixty laps—the race was roaring by. I had to see if I had the horse under me I thought I had, one I could actually ride to the front of the pack. If the handling was right and I was doing everything I knew how to do and I still couldn't get there, then that would be a real concern for me. I wouldn't be in control of my own destiny. I would be just another car in the crowd. I knew that as soon as I got my car handling right and I decided it was time to go, I'd better start gaining some ground. Oh, and I did.

Draft, block, pass: It really wasn't so complicated. That's what I'd been doing my whole life. And I was doing it again. Weaving through the traffic and moving up a car at a time.

The block part of the technique used to win at Daytona is interesting. Everybody does it. You block for two reasons. One is the obvious reason: to keep someone from passing you. But the second reason is at least as important as the first one: so you can get a push from the guy following you. Two cars hooked up at Daytona go way faster than one. You block. The guy pushes. You speed up. It's a wonderful thing.

By the time we hit lap 70, I had raced to the front of the pack. I was leading the Daytona 500, driving for Dale Earnhardt. It felt great. But there was a lot of race left to go. Don't get ahead of yourself, Mikey, I thought.

Things were going perfectly—so far. I'd definitely learned I had a car I could win the race in. I'd gotten the adjustment I needed. I'd been patient long enough. I'd absorbed the flow of the race. When I was ready to go, I went. From lap 70 to lap 170, I was at or near the front most of the way. I didn't lead much, but I led some. And I was certainly competitive through the whole middle part of the race.

With thirty laps to go, things were getting really intense. This is to be expected so late in such a big race. With every lap that goes by after the halfway point, the intensity ratchets up a notch. Early in the race, if you were thinking about trying to squeeze into a tight hole, you might say, "Ah, I'd better not try that." Now it was getting down to where if you needed to squeeze yourself into a hole, you were going to squeeze in there—or try, anyway.

When people start squeezing into holes and taking chances like that, that's when crashes occur. And when crashes happen at tracks like Daytona and Talladega, the restrictor-plate racetracks, the crashes usually involve a whole bunch of cars at once. At plate races, pretty much everybody on the track is in that same draft.

On this day at Daytona, there were thirty-some cars in this lead draft. The front of that pack is the safest place to be. At lap 172, I made it to the front again. At lap 173, I was very glad I had.

Coming off turn two, somebody tried to get in a hole that wasn't there. There was a major crash. More than twenty cars involved. A serious, race-altering pileup on the back straightaway. When I looked in my mirror, there was stuff flying everywhere. One car was even flipping, doing cartwheels back there. Smoke, dirt, parts, pieces—what a mess! What a crash!

Back in 2001, even more so than now, you worried anytime you saw any wreck, especially one of this magnitude. Part of your brain always thinks, Someone could be hurt back there. Could be someone I'm close to. Heck, it just as easily could have been me. But at the same time, there is also relief. Your car's not torn up. You can race. It's really nice when the big crash is behind you or you weave your way through it somehow.

I was looking in the mirror seeing all these cars wrecking behind me, and I was thinking: I hope everyone's okay. For sure, that took a bunch of guys' chances away.

The caution flag flew, and it was quickly replaced by the red. The wreck was so big, NASCAR didn't want us driving back through all the debris. Besides, the ambulances needed to get to all the cars that were crashed to make sure no one was injured. Whenever there's a red flag, the field is brought to a stop just past the start-finish line. As we rolled to a stop, I was looking in my mirror to see how many cars had actually made it through the wreck, how many people I was now going to have to fight to win the Daytona 500. But what quickly caught my attention were the two cars directly behind me. One was red and one was black. It was Dale Junior and Dale, just like Dale had said it would be.

Dale Junior and I were ahead of the wreck. Dale had somehow weaved through it. Can you believe that?

I kept looking and finally thought: Where's Park? He wasn't around, just like Dale had said he wouldn't be. I mean, seriously? I know Dale's won seven championships and seventy-some races. But this was freaky. How did he know this? The three of us, one, two, three! It took me a minute to get my brain around that one.

Now we were working together for real. We didn't have to sort through forty other cars anymore to find each other. Most everybody had crashed. There were maybe fifteen of us left. And the three of us were up front. For the first time I could see it. I could see exactly what Dale was talking about. The three of us, up in the front. It was time to put our plan—Dale's plan—into action.

Line up and work together.

Once NASCAR lifted the red flag, we all made our way to Pit Road for the final stops of the race. I entered Pit Road as a leader but exited fourth. Dale Junior had taken the top spot, and Dale was third. The green flag waved on lap 179, and the field was cut in half. But I couldn't tell. The action at the front of the pack was more intense than it had been all day.

It was wild up there. We were all fighting to see who could get to the lead.

Sterling Marlin had a really fast car. He pushed his way to the front after the caution. But just a lap later, I grabbed the lead back from him.

Sterling was right on my bumper. Dale Junior and Dale were behind him. We needed to shake Sterling out of there. And with fourteen to go, that's what Dale and Dale Junior did.

Now we were one, two, three—all lined up at the front. Imagine that! Again, it was just like Dale had planned.

Thirteen laps from the finish. Talk about drama! But I had Dale Junior on my bumper, and no one could really get up to me. With eleven to go, Sterling got close. But our three cars tied together held him off. Junior and I were bumper to bumper at the front of the pack. The guy who had a real fight on his hands was Dale. He was in third, in a vulnerable position.

I was safe, I was hoping, because Dale Junior was latched onto me and was pushing. So I had a buffer between the action and me. Dale Junior was in a good position too, because Dale was pushing him. Dale was his buffer to all the people who were wanting to intrude on our little party at the front. Dale was third. He had no buffer. Nobody was pushing him. Fourth, fifth, sixth, all those other guys—they weren't just waiting around. They weren't sitting in line like Junior and I were. They were trying to fight their way up past Dale, press themselves into the action, and grab the lead. And they didn't have much time left.

As each lap passed and I held the lead, I kept wondering, "What's Junior thinking?"

The drama continued to build for me as each lap passed and I still held onto the lead. Holding it and keeping my eye on Junior.

As far as I was concerned, he was a wild card. I didn't really know Dale Junior. I believed what Dale had told me, that we would all work as a team—the three of us—and win the race together.

I believed it, but I didn't know it.

Dale Junior and I didn't have a relationship. If you had asked Junior, he would have said: "I don't know why my dad and Mike are friends. I just know they hang out all the time."

I think Dale Junior wondered what we had in common that made us friends. I was about halfway between their ages. Dale was forty-nine. I was thirty-seven. Dale Junior was twenty-something, just a kid. I was an old married guy with kids. Dale was too. So I had more in common with Dale than I did with Dale Junior. Like most fathers and sons, the two of them were at different places in life.

Junior had had a lot of attention cast on him since he first showed up in NASCAR. Being Dale Earnhardt's son meant the whole world was watching every pass he made. Dale Junior certainly hadn't disappointed anyone who hoped he could hold a steering wheel like his old man could. Championships in the Busch Series, winning in his rookie season in Cup, Junior was proving he could. But because of all the attention he had gained from driving a car, he put a shell around himself.

I know Dale was proud of Junior. Dale the dad would light up when talking about all his kids and their accomplishments.

Dale had told me I could count on Junior. Now he was right behind me. I hoped Dale was right. He certainly had been so far.

I drove my car ninety percent of the time with my eyeballs in the mirror. I ran all the final laps that way. It wasn't that I didn't trust what Dale had told me. It was that I had to make sure I did all I could do to keep Dale Junior right in my tire tracks. I'd never talked to him about any of this. And this was the Daytona 500. He was just a kid. What was he thinking? He knew the plan, didn't he? Would he do what his father told him to? I believed he would. Was I being naïve to think so? This was all new to me.

I sure wished I'd talked to Junior before the race to see where he was mentally, to hear those words directly from him.

That would have been a good idea, Mike. A little late now. Get over it.

Worrying about all that now was dumb. What was important was for me to focus on my car and keep myself positioned on the track the way I wanted to. If I hadn't been able to stay right on the bottom of the racetrack and I'd opened the door for Dale Junior to get in there, I bet he would have. He would've said: "You slipped up, and I had to go." That's how that would have gone down.

So it was really important for me to do my job, not to give him that opening. And that's what I did. I did my job exactly like I was supposed to do it. I did it perfectly. I never gave Dale Junior the room to make a move on me.

I just kept watching my mirror, and it kept looking just like Dale said it would. Dale Junior was right on my bumper. He was doing exactly what he was supposed to do. And behind him, Dale was moving around a lot. I could see Dale Junior, and there were times on the straightaways I could see Dale too. All those other drivers were drafting up on him. There was a lot going on back there. I could tell that.

The other drivers were getting their runs. They were trying to pass. First Sterling. Then Schrader. Rusty Wallace too. They were all trying to fight their way to the front. Their chances to gain ground on me and Junior were winding down. If they were ever going to get to us, they had to get around one of the fiercest competitors of all time. It seemed like Dale had drawn a line in the sand: "No way you're crossing this."

But as determined as he was to keep them from crossing it, they were equally determined to say, "What line?"

For anyone going mano a mano against Dale Earnhardt at Daytona, I'd bet on Dale Earnhardt every time. They were teaming up on him, and that made it a fairer fight for those guys, I guess. But they couldn't pass.

Dale was working, man. Blocking, crowding, getting run into and bounced off of, and drafting all over the place. He was doing all he could do to keep pushing us ahead. Dale said this is how it would be: Someone would get the lead and the other two would push.

But the more I've thought about it, the more I am sure: He wanted to be right where he was. I bet he didn't think Dale Junior or I could do the job he was doing. And he was probably right.

If either one of us had been in Dale's position, I don't think we would have been as good or disciplined or smart as he was at sticking to the plan. He knew he needed to be that guy. He stayed back there in third and fought and blocked and tried to keep all those people off us. He did just that. He did an amazing job.

At the same time, I was doing exactly what I was supposed to do. Once I got the lead, I wasn't just out for a Sunday drive. I had to be calculating. I had to be sharp. I didn't just run with my foot flat on the floorboard, although I could have. I knew that wouldn't get me the win. I had to recognize what was going on behind me. Going down the straightaway, I'd roll off the gas pedal just a little. I didn't want to get too far ahead of Dale Junior. If I'd gotten too far ahead of him, it would have given him the room to make a run if he wanted. The gap I would have put on him would have given him the momentum he needed to maybe pull out and pass me. I couldn't take anything for granted.

I know now that pulling out and making a move was the last thing he was going to do. He was just doing what he was told. He was staying in line. He was pushing me. But I didn't know all that then. If he'd told me that before the race—or I'd asked him—it would have made my life a whole lot easier. Or would it have? Would I have believed him? It doesn't matter. Bottom line is, at the time, I didn't know what he was thinking.

As the laps ticked down, nothing changed. I kept looking in my mirror thinking, Five to go. Dale Junior isn't making a move. He's still sitting right there.

My confidence was rising now. Time was running out.

"No one's made a run yet," I said to myself. "I don't think they're gonna get one now. I don't think it's gonna happen. They can't get to me."

At a moment like that, you have to keep your concentration no matter what happens on the track. As Dale had proven at Talladega in the fall, no race is over until the checkered flag.

"Okay, just race," I told myself. "Just race. Do your job. Stay in the present. Don't get ahead of yourself."

I watched the mirror and the track and made sure I stayed right where I was supposed to be, which was down on the bottom of the track.

I sat there and played with the gas pedal and kept myself spaced and did everything I was supposed to do in order to be in a position to win the race.

I knew what I was doing. And I was going to keep on doing it. I was in control of what I was doing. I just wished I knew what the guy in the red car was going to do.

CHAPTER 22

CHECKERED FLAG

I was a mess.

I was so close to winning the Daytona 500. I was out front. Just a few laps to go. And in my mirror, all I could see was red.

It said, "Bud." Well, actually, technically, from where I was looking, it said, "duB." It also said that objects in my mirror might be closer than they appeared, but I don't think this object could have been any closer. This duB was all over me.

Keep pushing, I thought. Keep shoving. Come on, Junior. We're almost there.

There wasn't much talk over the radio. Inside my car, all I heard was a word or two every now and then. "All clear," said Chuck, my spotter. "It's you and the eight, single file." The only voice in my head was Scott, my crew chief. He was counting down the laps. "Three to go," he said as I crossed the start-finish line again. There wasn't any coaching from anyone. I was in my world, focusing on doing the job Dale hired me to do.

"Two to go."

In the mirror, nothing much had changed. Dale Junior was right on my bumper. Dale looked like he was back there swatting flies. Next time by, they'd be waving the white. But the white in racing doesn't mean surrender. It means just the opposite. It means desperation for the other guys.

As we raced off turn four toward the white flag, I liked what I saw out back. I had lifted off the gas entering turn three and timed that lift perfectly. Dale Junior was right on my bumper, right where I wanted him to be. And behind Junior, Dale, Sterling, and Schrader were all in line. As we crossed the start-finish line again, Scott calmly said, "One to go. Bring her home, baby."

From what I was looking at behind me, I believed I was going to do just that. It didn't look as if anyone was lined up to make any kind of run. All the chaos of three wide and Dale blocking was gone when we went into turn one for the last time. Just five cars in a line. It wasn't nutty back there anymore. Was this the calm before the storm? Were those guys lining up to make one last assault?

They would have to make that last run on me off turn two. And when we came off the turn, I didn't see it. Junior was right on me, and the others were in line too. I thought, There's no way. There's no way they're gonna get me. If I can drive to the end of this straightaway, make two left turns and drive up that other straightaway, and my engine doesn't blow up and one of my tires doesn't blow out, I'm gonna win. They can't get me now.

At that point, it looked like we were playing Follow the Leader. But suddenly, about halfway down the back straightaway with Dale Junior right behind me, Sterling and Schrader made a run on Dale. They split him.

They were three wide when we went into turn three. This was good for me and Junior but not so good for Dale. I was right. I was going to win, and Dale Junior was going to be second, right on my bumper. Junior couldn't pass me. The three-wide battle behind him meant my win was secure.

However, the storybook one-two-three finish, the one it looked like we were getting ready to celebrate, was in jeopardy. The last time I could see what was going on back there, Dale was in a fight for third.

But I was coming off turn four now, and I was looking for something I'd never seen. I had turned my focus from the black and red cars that were pushing me to the black-and-white flag that was going to be mine. I was so focused on where I was headed, I was paying no attention to what was happening behind.

I didn't hear Chuck, the spotter, say: "They're crashing behind you."

My eyes were looking for that something I'd never seen before in Cup. And it was waving up ahead.

A checkered flag being thrown at me on a Sunday afternoon.

And this wasn't just any checkered flag. This one would say: Daytona 500.

"There it is," I yelled. "There it is!"

"Woo-hoo!"

"Yes, winner!"

"Woo-hoo! Yes!"

"Michael Waltrip is a winner!"

Finally, my 0-fer curse was over.

And there was Dale Junior right behind me in second. He hung in behind, just like his daddy said he would.

I noticed the caution lights were flashing. There must have been a wreck back there, I thought. But by then, I was slipping into a mild state of shock. All I could think was, We did it! We won the Daytona 500! Unbelievable!

I was in grade school when I started coming down here, gazing at the high banks of Daytona. Just looking at those banks is how I fell in love with this place. It's funny how a little boy could fall in love with asphalt. But I did. Now after sixteen years of chasing wins—heck, a win—in Cup, this one was real.

Daytona counts. It counts more than any race. This is the greatest race in the world. I would put this trophy right by the one I won at the All-Star Race. If you're only ever going to win two races, those were two pretty good ones.

As I continued around the track after the race, I drove right by that wreck Chuckie was talking about. There were crashed cars, ambulances, and safety workers at the scene. But I didn't notice any of that or pay it any attention. I was just staring straight ahead, trying to get my mind around what had just happened to me.

So many emotions.

I was happy, for sure. I was thankful. I was relieved. My eyes were full of tears. My brain was glazing over. But how could I miss something as huge as the aftermath of that wreck? There were ambulances everywhere down there. Wreckers. And Dale's car was right up in the middle of the accident.

I remember the cool-down lap clearly. I remember driving right past there. But none of it registered.

I'm thankful for that. I'm thankful for the moments of clueless celebration that followed. I knew I would get a chance to savor the love of my family, my team, and the huge throng of fans showing their appreciation of what we had just achieved, to bask in the celebration of my first win in NASCAR's greatest race. And that felt awesome.

For a while.

What if I had noticed that crash? What would I have done? Especially if I'd seen who was in it. God only knows. I probably would have stopped, gone over, helped Dale out of his car to get a big hug from him. As it was I just motored on by.

I believe the good Lord protected me from seeing that and sent me straight to Victory Lane.

There, everything would be magical. I would experience first-hand something I had only dreamed of. My family, my team, and friends, all of them, would be there. And none of them would even try to fight back the tears.

Why should they? My eyes were already full of tears. Tears of joy.

It had taken me years to get this party started. And I didn't have anything to do for a week. That's when the next race was. I wanted to celebrate till then.

CHAPTER 23

VICTORY LANE

There I was, on the most sought-after piece of real estate in all of motorsports, Victory Lane at Daytona. What a way to break a little losing streak, huh?

As soon as I pulled into Victory Lane in my #15 NAPA Chevy, everything in the world seemed perfect. Buffy was there, crying, laughing, smiling. I grabbed her and said, "We did it, baby! We won this race! We won it just like Dale said we would!"

The sound of roaring engines had now been replaced by the sound of a couple hundred thousand screaming fans, clapping and cheering for a guy who had been trying for sixteen years to win a race. Now he had won *the* race. Confetti was raining down on my head. Champagne and beer were being sprayed everywhere. This was incredible. Victory at Daytona.

We were living it up, sucking up the moment. I couldn't imagine that feeling would ever end.

This was my special time, although I didn't know how clueless I was. It was the greatest ever. We laughed and cheered and hugged. The celebration was under way, one I thought would last forever. Buffy, Macy, my family, my team—all of us were there, and all of us were winners. That dumb streak was over—finally! No more 0-fer. No more asterisk by my name. This win counted.

My heart was still racing. The adrenaline was still pumping through my veins. But of all the excitement and other emotions I was feeling, the one that felt the best was that relief. I was a winner. At last.

I wasn't especially tired. It wasn't a hot day. Daytona isn't really a physically challenging racetrack. It's very mentally taxing because of the large pack that you're racing in and how hard you have to focus in order to put yourself in the right position. But now that it was over, I could say my run to the checker had been calmer than most that I had been in. Out front was the place to be, and I'd never been there before. I was usually in the back, scratching and clawing to scrape out a top-five finish. But I'd focused on driving my car and watching my mirror and keeping an eye on what Dale Junior was doing behind me. We had a race plan. We followed it. I knew in my heart that given the opportunity, I would win. A lot of people said there was a lot of pressure on me now that I was driving Dale's car. But I disagreed. I thought having a ride like this would take the pressure off of me. Finally, I could just race to win. And I was right.

So instead of being overly exuberant, I was just more like, Thank God. I finally won a race. Any race. A race that counted. And this one counted a lot.

I looked up and there was Macy, standing near her mom. She had a huge smile on her face, and she gave me a hug as big as only a three-year-old can. It was a lot like the hugs she gave me in the motor home when this day first got started. Man, that seemed like a long time ago. She had a pretty dress on. She looked so beautiful and so proud. I kissed her on the forehead and held her tight. Then, just as I let go, one of the guys on the crew decided to take a beer can, shake it up, and squirt her, spraying a can of Budweiser all over Macy and her pretty little dress.

The dude was a bit too excited. He was caught up in the moment, I guess.

Macy didn't think this was funny at all. She let out a giant wail: "*Ah-hhhhh!*" The poor child was screaming like she was at the dentist. My niece, Dana, the nanny, was right behind her, quickly wiping off her beautiful little face. But I think Macy decided this Victory Lane place wasn't nearly as cool as the rest of us thought.

Well, at least it was the right beer, our sponsor's beer! Who doesn't like a good, cold duB?

Buffy was totally loving and supportive, as always. Hugging me, congratulating me—tears still running down her face. It was like she could hardly believe it. Everybody seemed to be crying except me. And I'm a crier. I do cry. But not now. I had shed a few tears in the car, and I was done. Happiness? Joy? All that? Sure. But mainly, I was just relieved.

Thank you, God. Thank you, Dale. Thank you, Dale Junior.

The whole crew was gathered around. Our sponsors were too, sharing this moment with the team. I was so happy for the folks from NAPA who had taken a chance on me when Dale asked them to just a few months before. Now they and all our other sponsors—Coca-Cola, Aaron's, Klaussner Furniture, and the others—were tasting victory with us. Most of the sponsors had already become our friends. This was their victory too.

Everybody was there. To celebrate. To take pictures. Just to be part of this incredible moment. A couple of the NASCAR reps were making sure the Victory Lane experience went down exactly like it was supposed to. They were making sure that the team was taken care of and the media were getting the interviews they needed.

That's what it was like for a while after I got out of the car. A thousand things needed to happen. As the driver, you're never going to remember everything unless someone is there to guide you. I know I wouldn't have. How would I know what to do? I'd never been there before.

Dick Berggren, pit reporter for Fox, quickly made his way to me. Dick had been around racing forever. I believe he was covering chariot racing when Ben-Hur was a rookie. (Hi, Dick.) He's a former driver himself. He had a pretty good notion of what I might be feeling at a moment like that. It was his job to be one of the ones who always reminded me I'd never won a race. And he did it again.

"Michael Waltrip," he said in a slightly serious tone, as if he were calling my name off a school-attendance roll or summoning me up to a witness stand. "Four hundred and sixty-two green flags, finally a checker. Does this feel as good as you hoped?"

Actually, Dick, 463! If you're going to call me out, get the number right!

Almost any driver will tell you he has fantasized about this moment a thousand times. You've just won the race. The crowd is roaring. The camera is rolling. The whole world is waiting to hear what you have to say. Make it count, baby! Make it count, Mike!

And I know how to tell a good story. People like all the stuff I go on with! So this was gonna be good, right?

You want to know the first words out of my mouth?

"It's unconscious."

Unconscious? Is that really what I said? I have no idea what that meant. I'm known as a talker. This was my moment! Finally, people wanted to hear what I had to say. And that's what I said? "It's unconscious"?

I then gathered myself and put together a few words that actually made sense, although I did stumble through them.

"Thank God," I started. "Thank my dad. I love him so much. And, um, you know, I just can't believe it. It hasn't, ah, sunk in yet." Well, that was deep! Keep it going, Mike. "I know I never would have won without Dale Junior. So he has to get half the credit. And I know I never would have won without the belief that Dale had in me and NAPA and all the people on my team."

My mind was racing. I knew my time was short. I had so much I wanted to get in.

"I thought it kind of boosterish—or bragging—that we thought we could win this race. We hadn't won any race yet. And we did win."

Berggren said my brother wanted to talk to me from the broadcast booth. Darrell was a mess. He was so happy for me and so emotional. He had just called his baby brother winning the Daytona 500. He didn't try to hide his feelings about that either. "Way to go!" he shouted at me and viewers around the country. "Way to go, buddy! Keep it low, Mikey. Keep it low. Don't let 'em run up on you. Come on, man. Come on, man. Block him. Block him. You got him, Mikey. You got him, man."

He turned to Mike Joy, exhausted, at the end. "My daddy would be so happy."

Quite a day for the Waltrips.

Now in Victory Lane, Berggren handed me a headset. Darrell's voice was loud and clear. We were talking in front of a huge television audience, millions of people watching around the world, including my proud momma back in Sherrills Ford. But when I heard him in the headset, it was like we were sitting on the back of the truck, just him and me.

"What's up, Brother?" I asked Darrell.

"Man, I want to be down with you," he said. "I want to give you a big hug. Man, way to go! I was riding with you. I was praying for you. Pulling for you."

By that point, it was just Darrell and me, telling a new family story, although I was doing most of the talking this time.

"Well, as soon as I find Dale Junior, I'm gonna give him a big kiss," I said. "He won me the race, and you can't do this deal nowadays without friends. He was my friend. His Budweiser Chevy ran second. He had a dream. He won the Daytona 500. And he did. I'm just here to celebrate, man."

I looked at Berggren. It was straight stream-of-consciousness now. "Can I say one more thing? *Woo-wee!*" I let out the loudest whoop I had inside me. "God, I can't believe it's over!" No more 0-fer.

Then it was back to Big Brother. I've always been a pretty big talker. Now I was kinda taking over the post-race interview. To his credit, Berggren was totally gracious, just giving me my space and my moment.

"Now let me ask you a question, Darrell," I went on. "How much better does one for 463 sound? Instead of 0 for 462?" I didn't really give him a chance to answer. "You people are hung up on my record," I said. "I don't care. But I do know this. Me and my brother have both won the Daytona 500!"

"That's right, Brother," Darrell said. "That's right, brother. Tell 'em about it. Get up on that car." I would. In a minute. But first I had so many people to thank. And of course, at a time like that, your mind is constantly blanking out on you. You can never think of half of them.

"All my friends," I said. "Golly, Scott Eggleston. There are so many people, Dick. On and on. I'm gonna have lots of time to thank people."

Couldn't forget my mom, though.

"Momma, I love you. Momma, I wish you were here. Golly, if my daddy were here, it would be complete. This is a day the Lord has made. And I'm proud, and I never gave up. You know, you can't win if you give up. I didn't care how many 0-fers I had. I showed up every Sunday and did my job. And today I finally won one of these things."

"Michael, you know how much money you won?" Darrell asked.

"There ain't no telling," I said.

"A million dollars! You won a million dollars! You are a millionaire!"

Even at that moment, I knew that race money never quite added up like you thought it would. Good thing Darrell wasn't my owner. He'd probably send me another check for a thousand and keep the rest.

"The last time I won a lot of money," I said, "I won the All-Star Race. It paid two hundred thousand. I got half of that, and I said, 'I'm gonna build my momma and daddy a house.' That cost a hundred grand. The government got half of mine. I went fifty thousand in the hole. I'm not making any promises today."

Before I got done, I had one more thing I needed to say, something that I guess was obvious, but I wanted it to be heard coming out of my mouth: how much I had benefited from the help of Dale and Dale Junior and the whole DEI racing crew.

"I can't believe it," I said. "I owe it all, or most of it, to Dale Junior. He helped me a lot. And his daddy too. I saw him back there fighting them off. I know they're both real proud of me, their driver, but more importantly this team they threw together for a few months. They hired me to drive it and people were like, 'Why'd he do that? He must really like him.' Well, this is why he did that. Because I knew I could do this job. This is why he did it."

I hugged and kissed Buffy and Macy, saw all my family who were there in Victory Lane. I even talked to my brother on TV. But the one guy I was sure was on his way to join our celebration, the one I wanted to see the most, the one I was sure would give me a bear hug I would never forget—I hadn't seen him yet.

"Hey, y'all. Where's Dale?"

PART 4:
DEALING WITH IT

CHAPTER 24

THE COVERAGE

Mike Joy was the lead announcer in the broadcast booth, calling the race for Fox. As I was roaring toward the checkered flag, Mike turned his eyes away from me and Dale Junior for a moment and the victory that was about to be ours. That's when millions of TV viewers got their very first indication that something had gone wrong.

"Big trouble!" the veteran race announcer warned. "Big! Right behind them!"

As Mike, Darrell, and Larry McReynolds described the action, I was in my own little world, rolling down the track at 190 miles an hour, ticking off the last few seconds of NASCAR's Great American Race, on my big day. I was focused on the checkered flag in front of me.

At home, the TV audience could hear my brother Darrell cheering me toward the checker. "To the flag!" he yelled. "Come on, Mikey! You got it! You got it! Mikeeeeey! All right! All right!" But as three glorious words moved across Mike Joy's lips—"Michael Waltrip wins!"—the story of the 2001 Daytona 500 was going to get more complicated by the second. Nobody had any idea yet how complicated.

The scene at the finish was still the main story. For now, it was. But some very unsettling developments were starting to intrude.

Two cars had hit the wall between turns three and four of the final lap. That was clear from the video. These were Kenny Schrader's and Dale Earnhardt's cars. They bounced off the wall and spun around, then slid through the final-lap traffic into the infield.

Quickly, Kenny could be seen climbing out of his yellow #36 M&M's

Pontiac and rushing toward Dale's black #3 Goodwrench Chevy. From a distance, it was impossible to see inside Dale's car as Kenny and then an ambulance crew made their way to him. But one thing was for sure: Dale wasn't climbing out. And the guys in the broadcast booth had a race to recap. Two important story lines were beginning to collide.

My brother Darrell, who'd finally caught his breath from yelling "Go, Mikey" so many times, was the first one to ask. "How 'bout Dale? Is he okay?"

For Darrell to ask a question like that, he had to have suspicions. Darrell wasn't new to scary-looking crashes. He'd seen many of them over the years. One second, he was crying tears of joy, cheering his baby brother to the checkered flag. The next, those tears still in his eyes, he was turning his attention to turn four, where Dale's car had come to a stop. "How 'bout Dale? Is he okay?" At that moment, no one really knew the answers to those questions. But Darrell knew he didn't like what he saw.

What a swing of emotions my brother faced right there. Out of one eye, he could see me celebrating with my team in Victory Lane. Out of the other, he could see the emergency medical teams rushing toward Dale. Eventually, Darrell knew, I was going to find out what had happened over there. What a gut-wrenching position—on live TV.

He and his colleagues had to gather themselves. The show had to go on. Darrell was no longer just my brother or Dale Earnhardt's friend. He had another job to do. Now he and his colleagues were reporters with a complicated story to tell.

"Schrader has climbed out of his car," Mike Joy said, repeating all that anyone knew yet. "He and Dale Earnhardt crashed between turns three and four." Then, changing gears quickly, Mike asked: "Darrell, is this better than winning it?"

"This is great," Darrell said. "I just hope Dale is okay. I guess he's all right, isn't he?"

It was clear that nobody knew much of anything yet, least of all me. Mike Joy was doing some TV housekeeping, recapping the finish of the race.

"Now, Earnhardt and Schrader did not complete the final lap," he noted. "So they're scored at 199 laps, along with Robert Presley, Brett

Bodine, Kyle Petty, and on back through the rest of the field. These results are unofficial."

Darrell spoke again. He couldn't keep his attention off turn four.

"As excited as I am for Michael and proud as I am of him," my brother said, "I'm just, I'm praying for Dale. He's back down there, and they're working down there. So we need to worry about him."

The two competing stories—one bright and cheery, the other dark and unknown—were pushed and pulled through the rest of the telecast. At times, Mike Joy was just following the script, for instance, after a break when he said: "Chevy congratulates Michael in the #15 Monte Carlo." At other moments, the emotion was impossible to hold back. When the helicopter shot showed the ambulance pulling away from Dale's wrecked car, Mike, Darrell, and the rest of the Fox team bounced back and forth with their competing narratives.

"Dale Earnhardt was removed from his car, and you see the ambulance transporting him directly to Halifax Medical Center in Daytona Beach, which fortunately is but two miles from the Speedway," Mike said. "That's all the news we have. If we don't get a further update on Earnhardt's condition during our telecast, tune in to *Victory Lane* at 9 P.M. on Fox Sports Net tonight."

With the help of video replays the Fox guys tried to figure out how the wreck might have occurred. Larry McReynolds wondered whether Rusty Wallace's car had bumped Dale or not. They worked their way through it.

"Darrell," Larry said, "it looked like when Rusty run up there through the middle, it maybe just took the air off Dale's spoiler. It don't look like anyone got into him at all."

Or had someone? What about Sterling Marlin?

"Sterling may have gotten into it just a teeny bit and got him headed up the hill," Darrell said. "It's hard to say. Those kinds of licks are the worst kind. They're sudden."

Whatever. When the video was played again, the impact of the accident looked pretty severe.

"Schrader was riding him into the wall," Darrell said, sounding increasingly concerned. "So you get the impact of not only one car, but two cars. It looks like right there—"

"Looks like maybe he did get into it," McReynolds agreed.

"Sterling got into him, and here he goes," Darrell continued. "Man, not only is he going into the wall, but he's got Schrader riding in there with him."

"Lucky they didn't take another six cars with them," Mike Joy said.

"I don't like that," Darrell said. "That's not the kind of crash—" He didn't finish that sentence, as if he didn't want to say, "That's not the kind of crash you survive." The way Darrell put it was: "That's the kind of crash that hurts you."

Jeanne Zelasko, a pit reporter on the Fox broadcast team, grabbed Kenny Schrader as he came out of the Infield Care Center, where he'd been checked out and quickly released. Kenny was talking with a group of reporters when Jeanne pushed in.

"Someone runs into someone for no reason," Kenny said. "That's all. I mean the rules are fantastic. They've really got a good rules package."

When the pit reporter asked about Dale's condition, Kenny didn't offer much.

"I don't really know," he said. "I'm not a doctor. I got the heck out of the way as soon as they got there."

"How 'bout yourself, how are you?" one of the reporters asked.

"I'm fine, I'm fine," he said. "Just thinking about Dale."

"Take us through it," the reporter pressed.

"I don't know what happened," Kenny said again. "All of a sudden, we was all crashing. It started behind me. But I got part of it."

For now, that would have to be it. No one who really knew what was going on was talking. The people who were talking didn't know much. As I continued my Victory Lane celebration, no one was telling me anything. I was just readying myself for whatever was coming next. The broadcast was ending. Time was running out. Mike Joy and his colleagues did their Daytona 500 wrap-up.

"While Dale's driver Michael Waltrip celebrates," Mike said in what turned out to be a fairly good summary of where things stood, "Dale Earnhardt rides in the back of an ambulance to the Halifax Medical Center. It is the emotions of this sport. It is the irony of Daytona."

With each minute that passed, it was getting more obvious to viewers: These guys on TV were juggling triumph and tragedy.

"All right," said Chris Myers, who had anchored the pre-race broadcast and was now closing the show. "It's the kind of day that a motion picture could certainly cover here. Michael Waltrip becomes the sixth driver in history to have his victory, the Daytona 500—after 462 races—become his first win. He comes away with the victory."

I agree, Chris. The story of that February afternoon in Daytona—how I got there and how I left—had more than enough drama to fill a movie screen.

Ken Squier had been covering the Daytona 500 as a journalist since before I ever raced there. He was the announcer when CBS first aired live flag-to-flag coverage in 1979. He had the perspective of history.

"A couple of thoughts as we get down to the end of today," Ken said. "William Manchester has written that true heroism is not based on a single incident, but is built on courage and commitment in the face of the unknown and potential danger over time. Heroes are those who are unwavering to their calling, said Manchester. So we've seen a winner today.

"A young hero named Michael Waltrip and his four hundred and sixty-third start," Squier said, getting downright poetic here and quoting me. "He once said, 'No one owes me anything in this sport. I've been close, I've been competitive, so I am proud of these things. I love driving these cars and I want to do it for a long time to come.' The voice of a hero."

"The interesting thing is," Ken went on, finally wrapping up, "these heroes are not only today. They are heading for Rockingham next week and Las Vegas the week after. That is the mark of a true race and a true hero."

Dale was in an ambulance, taking a slow ride to the hospital. I was still in Victory Lane, wondering when he would come see me. The viewers were left hanging, unsure of how these two stories would eventually connect.

And with that Fox signed off from Daytona.

CHAPTER 25

BAD HINTS

O f course, I hadn't seen any of the TV coverage. I was still blissfully clueless. Although Dale hadn't gotten to Victory Lane yet, I knew he must be on his way.

I had it all figured out.

I guessed he got a piece of that last-lap wreck and was being checked out at the Infield Care Center. I could not wait until he got there and joined our celebration. He had to be so proud.

I mean, this win was more his than it was mine. He was why this all happened. He saw it happening way before I did, way before anyone did. He believed I could win all along, even before he hired me. He coached me all winter, and he directed the preparation of my #15 cars. Then, that meeting Friday. Wow! He called it! He called it and we did it!

I had it all pictured in my mind, him walking up with that mischievous grin all over his face that seemed to say, "Hey, I told you so. Hell, I told everyone so."

I wanted a hug, too. One like he had given Dale Junior when Junior won the All-Star Race in 2000. That was one of those moments that made me cry. And I wasn't even there when it happened. I'd just seen it on TV. But I knew how much it meant to the two of them.

I knew Dale, and I knew joy when I saw it, and that moment in Victory Lane with his son was joyous. I was about to receive that same type of approval, the I-knew-you-would-win-for-me validation I desperately needed. So as all the accolades of winning the Daytona 500 were being showered on me I kept wondering, Where's Dale?

I kept glancing at the entrance of Victory Lane. I was sure that any moment Big E was going to walk through there and give me what I wanted more than a trophy or a check. He was going to walk in there, start slapping everybody on the back, and say, "This is why all of you are on my team. I knew all of you were winners."

While the photographers took pictures and I smiled, I wondered: So what's taking Dale so long to get here?

He probably stopped to see Dale Junior. Junior did just finish second in the Daytona 500. Dale Earnhardt, the seven-time Cup Series champion driver, now could add owner of the first- and second-place finishers, a one-two finish, in the Daytona 500, to his impressive résumé. A lot of reporters probably wanted to talk to him about that.

Meanwhile, I was still doing interviews, posing for pictures, swapping hats, all the stuff I'd watched other people do for the past sixteen years, and I was loving every minute of it. It was my time to shine, and my smile was bigger than it had ever been. This scene would be complete as soon as Dale showed up.

I hope Dale Junior comes with him too, I was thinking. The three of us did this together. What could be better than the three of us being together in Victory Lane?

Man, where were they?

Heck, when I won the All-Star race, Dale was one of the first people to Victory Lane to congratulate me. He even beat my brother there. And Dale was only partly responsible for that win. He just put me and Wood Brothers together. He set it up. But we had to do the rest on our own. But not today. He put me in his car. He told me how we were going to win the race. And on the track, he made sure it all went down just like he said.

Between looking for Dale, I was still living in the hectic pace of Victory Lane. "Smile here, Mike." "Smile there, Mike." "Talk to Fox Dallas, Mike." "Talk to the local Fox affiliate, Mike."

But still no Dale.

I was beginning to grow a bit frustrated. I asked Buffy, Ty, and a couple of crew guys to find out where Dale was and why he wasn't there yet. They all told me similar things. "He's on his way. . . . He'll be here in a minute." And I bought that. Maybe Dale was giving me time to enjoy win number one with my new team. But that didn't make any sense. This was his new team too. I couldn't figure out why he wasn't there.

It seemed like he would have had plenty of time to be checked out at the track hospital, then stop to congratulate Dale Junior and make it here by now. But I just kept trying to justify why he wasn't there yet. I knew every reporter in Daytona would like to hear an answer from maybe the greatest NASCAR racer ever, winner of the 1998 Daytona 500 and some seventy other races: "How did you take a guy who had gone 0 for 462, put him behind the wheel, and have him go one for one? How did you do that, Dale? How's that possible?"

And I wanted to ask Dale the same thing. "How did you do that?" Clearly, it wasn't just an accident. You did it. "You planned it, and you made it happen today."

Finally, somebody I knew turned up.

It was Kenny Schrader. He'd been out there in the middle of all that mess with me. And now, I assumed, he came to say congratulations. When I saw Schrader coming toward me, I thought of my first win with the team I started behind my house. I beat him in a NASCAR West race in Colorado. We battled door to door, and I pulled away at the end. When I got to the airport that night, he'd written a note and stuck it on my plane.

"You are a wiener!" he wrote. "Congratulations, friend."

Kenny and I were buddies, and it was great to see him walking into Victory Lane. I had a trophy in my hand, confetti on my head, and a can-you-believe-this look on my face.

I said, "Schrader, look. I won the Daytona 500."

But this Kenny Schrader I was looking at, he didn't look right. And he wasn't acting right either. Certainly not the way I had expected him to. He should have been smiling, I thought. He must have been having trouble putting the moment into words.

"I know this is a bit of an upset," I joked. "But is it really that shocking that I actually won a race? You're speechless?"

Then he reached out and grabbed me, squeezing both my arms below my elbows. I didn't understand what he was doing. He didn't say a word. But I could tell he was upset.

"What's wrong?" I asked.

Kenny had his M&M's hat pulled way down over his eyes and giant sunglasses covering most of his face. This wasn't a familiar Schrader look to me. It was like he was hiding behind a mask. And the way he grabbed my arms was confusing to me.

Then, speaking softly, Kenny said three words I'll never forget.

"It's not good."

Kenny and I had a great relationship. We kidded each other all the time. Mainly he kidded me about not winning a race. But I knew he loved me, and it didn't bother me coming from him.

Again, he said, "It's not good. I think Dale's hurt."

His voice was shaking. He'd seen Dale in the car. "He's really hurt," Kenny said. He was being my friend, and he wanted me to be prepared for what I would learn next.

Schrader hugged me and said: "I love you, bud"—and then he walked off.

I know it took a lot of courage for Kenny to come and tell me that. It had to be hard. And think about what he was going through: He was racing to win the Daytona 500 on the last lap. I'm sure he could taste victory too. Then he was swept up in a wreck. When his car stopped, he was hurting, but he struggled out and saw Dale's car next to his and went to check on him.

Dale and Kenny were good friends too. Dale had helped Kenny get his feet under him when he moved to North Carolina back in the eighties to chase his racing dreams. Dale had helped Kenny the way Richard Petty had helped me. Dale gave Kenny advice and direction. Before you knew it, Schrader, a dirt racer from Missouri, was rubbing fenders with Dale in NASCAR. In 1984, Kenny was Rookie of the Year.

So Kenny was going over to help a friend out of his wrecked race car, something we'd all done before. He expected when he got there and dropped Dale's window net that they'd laugh about who won the race and all the crazy stuff that had gone on. I'm sure Kenny thought he'd lean in and lighten up the moment. He certainly didn't think he would lean in and see what he saw.

What he saw was Dale lying there, slumped over, unconscious. It knocked Kenny back. And he quickly started waving his arm, desperately calling for medical help.

All this was happening as I drove by heading to Victory Lane. As I was standing in Victory Lane, selfishly wanting Dale to come tell me what a great job I'd done, he was probably already dead. And the guy who got there first was Kenny. Now he was the first again, the first who tried to prepare me for how serious Dale's wreck really was.

It was becoming obvious this wasn't about me anymore. All that mattered now was Dale and his accident. I didn't know exactly how bad it was yet, but I didn't like the direction things were heading.

CHAPTER 26

IT'S REAL

While I was smiling and enjoying my victory, things were going on around me I was totally unaware of. Buffy knew. And she was working behind the scenes, coordinating who was going where when we left Victory Lane. She sent Dana and Macy to the hotel. She told my sister Connie and Connie's husband, Dave, that the two of us needed to be alone. They all left. So did Buffy's parents. They took Caitlin with them.

At the same time, someone from NASCAR was telling me it was time to go up to the suites and toast my victory with some NASCAR folks and some more sponsors. But I was getting fed up. Between Schrader coming to Victory Lane and me getting all those blank stares about Dale, I knew that something wasn't right.

A toast? I thought. I don't want a toast. I'm going to my bus.

"Buffy," I said, "let's go to the motor home."

The van that was going to take us to the suites took us to the coach lot instead. It was maybe a three-minute ride, the first time Buffy and I had been alone together since we got up that day.

As we settled into the van, I looked at her, and she just shook her head. She didn't say a word. She didn't have to.

When we got to the motor home, Buffy and I walked inside. It was empty, just the two of us. I had a strong idea what I was going to hear from her. And it wasn't going to be good.

With the last shred of hope I could muster, I asked, "He's gonna be okay, right?"

I knew in my mind Dale was hurt. My hope was he at least was still alive.

With that, Buffy began to cry. Through the sobs, she struggled to say the words I dreaded most: "Dale is dead."

I reached over and grabbed her, and I didn't want to let go. Then she said, "I'm so sorry, honey. You don't deserve this. Nobody does."

With Buffy in my arms and thoughts of how-could-this-be-happening running through my head, we just sat there and cried, thinking about our loss. Thinking about Teresa and the family. What it must be like for Dale Junior. Dale's mom back home in North Carolina. Everyone on the team, everybody in NASCAR, was going to be devastated by this.

Buffy and I sat together in the motor home where we had started our day. So much had changed in the last twelve hours.

When I woke up that morning, it was all about winning. Winning was all I could think of. Now I didn't want to think about winning at all. The day was now about a terrible loss. I just wanted to sit there, hold my wife, and cry.

And that's what I did.

For a long time, we didn't speak. We just stared off into the distance. What could we say? It was way too early to try to explain or justify. I just kept asking myself and asking God: "Why? Why? Why?"

Back in Bristol, when my dad was there and I wanted to win so badly for him, I blamed God when I didn't. I questioned why he couldn't let Dad and me celebrate that night. Then a month later, when we got the big win in Charlotte, I felt ridiculous for blaming God. I promised I would never do that again.

But there I sat a year and a half later, and I was on the verge of blaming God again.

But there is a big difference between blaming and asking. And who else could I ask? Where were the answers? This seemed so unlikely, so unfair.

But no one could answer my question. As I looked around, I realized I had so much to be thankful for, especially all the people who surrounded me. They went to work immediately, making sure I got through this as well as anyone could. Buffy, managing all the information and giving me a shoulder to cry on. Ty helping Buffy come up with a plan.

Schrader coming to give me a heads-up like he did. All these people came to me because they loved me, and I couldn't have gotten through it without them.

As Buffy and I collected ourselves, people began showing up to share their condolences with us. My brother Darrell and his wife, Stevie. My teammate Steve Park. Dale Jarrett. When NASCAR president Mike Helton was able to pull away from the hospital, he too came by.

Lying in bed that night, I was reflecting on the journey I'd shared with Dale. I was also thinking about my dad: how he'd been distant when I was little and we'd grown so close over the years. About his brave battle with lung cancer. About the day in Bristol when I got beat but Dad was still so proud of me. And the big win for my dad in Charlotte. Then at the end, him feeling like I didn't understand the pain of his illness as he died slowly in my arms.

After wallowing in all that emotion for hours, I reminded myself that I was a Christian. I believe everything does indeed happen for a reason. God does have a plan, although sometimes it's hard to understand. I decided that I needed to share that with the world, tell a positive tale about Dale's faith. If I could be positive, it would honor God. In my mind, two things were clear: It was Dale's day to go. And I was the perfect person to win that race that day.

The more I thought about it like that, the more sense it made to me. If some other guy had won, he would have wanted to grab credit for himself, credit for his team. That would have been completely understandable. He'd have had every right to feel that way. We are talking about the Daytona 500 after all. But I could use my position as the 500 winner to honor Dale. My team was Dale's team. He was as responsible for me winning as I was.

It was Dale's time to go, and I was the perfect person to give him credit for what we had accomplished together. I wanted to comfort all those who were hurt by telling them about the Dale I knew. My voice was certainly more relevant after what had happened that day than it had ever been before. So I had to embrace the opportunity to help others.

I had gone to bed that night with the crappiest attitude you could possibly imagine. Why, God? Why me? Again. How unfair it was to Dale! How unfair it was to me! But I fixed all that. I woke up the next day with a fresh view and the most positive attitude anyone could have had in a situation like that.

"I'm gonna honor Dale," I said to myself that Monday morning. "I'm gonna think of that as my responsibility from now on. To comfort people. To help make others feel as at peace with the loss of Dale as I possibly can."

CHAPTER 27

DAY AFTER

On the day after the Daytona 500, the winner heads up to New York for a couple of days of media attention, stopping by the *Today* show and *Live with Regis and Kelly* and some of the other shows. He gets to listen as everyone tells him how great he is. But my job that Monday was different. No New York City. No *Letterman* for me.

I was mentally ready and personally okay with tackling what lay ahead. One of my first responsibilities was to speak at a post-race press conference in Daytona and afterward head back to North Carolina to attend a funeral for a dear friend. It was so unnatural. I told myself I was going to make the most of this unimaginable situation. When something so unexpected happens, there is no way to be adequately prepared.

In the NASCAR world, the blame game had already begun. Fans were asking, "Earnhardt's dead? How could that be? Whose fault was the wreck?"

"Sterling Marlin hit Dale," people were saying. "He caused it. It was his fault."

Nothing could have been further from the truth. Man, we were just racing cars, racing for the biggest win in NASCAR. It was crazy to blame Sterling Marlin for this. But that's exactly what some people were beginning to do. I didn't understand it. It was wrong. Sterling was just racing, racing exactly like Dale would have. But fans were heartbroken. Their hero had been taken from them and they wanted someone to blame. Things got so ugly that Daytona track security and the Florida state police had to keep a special eye on Sterling. And back home in North

Carolina the local police stationed a squad car outside his shop in Moores-ville after a threat was phoned in.

But no way was Sterling responsible for Dale's death.

Dale's car spun out as he tried to protect Dale Junior and me, waging a four-way battle for third with Kenny Schrader, Rusty Wallace, and Ster-ling and trying to keep the other cars back. Sterling's car touched Dale's. But that's what happens in NASCAR, especially when the checkered flag is waving.

Sterling wanted to speak out. He wanted people to know he was hurt-ing too. He wanted to get on top of the situation in a hurry. He left Day-tona right away and headed home to Columbia, Tennessee. When he got there, he went to a newspaper office near his house and answered questions from the media.

"I'd do anything not to be here today addressing this topic," he said. "The focus should be on the Earnhardt family." But with all the uproar about him and his role in the crash, he said, "It appears that it would be best if I talked."

He'd been as surprised as anyone, he said, at the severity of the ac-cident. "We didn't know it was that bad." His team manager gave him the first heads-up. "Tony Glover told me about the time we were get-ting ready to leave the racetrack that it didn't look good for Earn-hardt. I said, 'Well, what do you mean?' He said, 'He's hurt pretty bad.'

"By the time we got to the airport," Sterling said, "they came and told us. I was in total shock. It made you just want to go throw up . . . just sick to your stomach."

But it was, after all, an accident. "It was strictly a racing accident," he said. "Things happened and people are going to look for somebody to blame. On a short track, you beat and knock and get by somebody, and they're going to pop you. But with them high-speed tracks, you know you don't touch anybody because you know it's going to hurt when you hit. No way in this world would I do something like that, knowing the consequences."

It was good that Sterling spoke up. But I thought it was important that the rest of us speak up too, to show that we didn't blame any driver for Dale's death. At that post-race press conference at Daytona on Monday, no one denied there'd been contact between Sterling's and Dale's cars. But a little contact is inevitable in a tight race, I said.

"Sterling didn't do anything wrong," I said. "Sterling was simply racing. When the checkered flag's waving, nobody is going to let off. When they rubbed, I'm sure Sterling didn't think Dale would wreck. Otherwise he wouldn't have rubbed him. But there was just a little bit of contact, and maybe it would have just shot Dale up the hill a little bit, Sterling probably thought, and he could make the pass.

"It's the last lap, it's racing. I don't think the wreck looked to me a result of anything other than guys wanting to get to the checkered. I believe that in my heart, and I hope that people will remember Sterling during this time."

Sterling seemed relieved at the support he received from his peers. "When your fellow drivers call," he said later, "and NASCAR calls and all the folks at DEI and Childress call and say, 'Man, just hold your head up. There's nothing you could have done,' it makes me feel a ton better."

Meanwhile, NASCAR officials were being pressed by the media for answers. Answers about the sport's safety record and how it was going to be improved. Wasn't Dale the fourth NASCAR driver to be killed in a crash in less than a year? Remember Adam Petty, the little boy I used to let sit in my lap and drive? Kyle's kid? He was making his way up the NASCAR ladder and was killed in a crash in 2000. Two other up-and-comers, Kenny Irwin Jr. and Tony Roper, were also killed that year.

We thought we were racing the safest cars in the world, but the sport was getting more dangerous. I once assumed when there was a crash, everyone would walk away. But more often now, people didn't. Racing was getting scary.

Was this a coincidence? Or had something changed? What was different? We know now—or at least I believe—the reason had to do with some advances in race-car engineering.

During the 1990s, racing teams developed a better technical understanding of the cars than we'd ever had before. When I started racing, I never heard of an engineer working on a race car. Back at BAHARI, we hired an engineer. But he mostly was just our travel agent, planning the trips where we would go testing. We didn't actually let him work on anything.

But in the 1990s, engineering became a routine part of how the cars were built. The teams learned and proved through testing that a more rigid car was a faster car. Not only was it faster, it was also more tunable. The stiffer the car's frame, the more effective adjustments became.

You go barreling into a bank turn at 200 miles an hour, stuff's gonna give. The frame is going to flex. Components that we thought were staying within .25 of an inch of tolerance were actually moving significantly more than that when the car was loading up in the banks.

The engineers' conclusion: "Stiffen 'em up. We gotta keep these frames from flexing. We gotta keep these components from moving. We'll get better results."

And they were right. Chalk one up for engineering. The rigid cars were performing better. Lap times were improving. We were all going faster. But people were getting killed.

The stiffness made the cars respond differently in accidents. This is Physics 101. Irresistible force meets immovable object. All that energy has to go somewhere. Before, the energy was spread throughout the whole floppy car. Now, because of that lap time everyone wanted so badly, that wasn't happening anymore. The stiffer car frame was giving less.

Think about that for a second. The walls are concrete. They hadn't given in the history of time and they weren't going to start giving now. With the car frames becoming less flexible, they weren't giving nearly as much as they used to. So before, when you hit a concrete wall, the wall didn't give but the car did. Now neither one of them was.

So where was all that energy going? Straight to the driver.

That's why I think Dale's accident was so deadly.

"There are no easy answers," said NASCAR CEO Mike Helton. NASCAR would move, but not rush. "We will not give up on looking for that new technology," he said on Monday in Daytona. "But in the meantime we simply are not going to react for the sake of reacting. We are not going to do something just because it's a reaction that we can take credit for. We will do it when it's the right thing to do."

It was understandable to second-guess NASCAR from the outside looking in. Cars were crashing and people were getting hurt. That's what the media and the public saw. But exhaustive research was already well under way. NASCAR's focus was on a couple of new technologies. One of them involved retaining walls that would help soften the blow when a car hit. These are called SAFER barriers, for Steel and Foam Energy Reduction. It's pretty simple how it works. A steel barrier is attached to a concrete wall. There's about a one-foot gap between the concrete and the steel. Foam is slipped in there. When a car hits the steel, the foam gives and the wall flexes. Basically, it's the same reason boxers wear gloves.

The other focus was on the HANS device. HANS stands for Head and Neck System. It was pretty simple too. A special collar was fitted to the driver. It sat over his shoulders and under his seat belts. This collar was attached to his helmet, stabilizing his head when he ran into something.

Sometimes genius is simple, isn't it?

Helton defended the progress NASCAR had already made and vowed continued improvements. "We've gone from no walls at all to wooden barriers to guard rails to concrete barriers," he said. "There very well may be a new substance out there that replaces concrete. We have not found it yet. Concrete still is the best barrier that can be incorporated in a racetrack."

Helton noted that the racing sanctioning body wasn't opposed to the HANS device. "NASCAR recommends drivers try it and work with the developers of it to perfect it for stock-car racing," he said. "It's a joint effort by every mind in the NASCAR garage to make all these elements work right."

Dr. Steve Bohannon, who tried to save Dale's life as he sat slumped in the wreckage, wasn't calling for mandatory HANS devices either. "Even if he had the device on," Bohannon said, "hitting the wall that fast may have resulted in the same injuries."

Dr. Bohannon continued, "Even if you restrain the head and neck in this type of injury with the forces we're talking about—hitting a concrete barricade at 150, 170 mph, whatever, there's still one more element you have to address," he said. "And that is the body has internal organs that are free-floating. The brain is floating in fluid, the heart, the liver are all floating inside the body. Even if you restrain the body—the head, the neck, the chest—all those organs internally still move in that kind of impact. The brain will still impact on the inside portion of the skull, and there's considerable forces involved."

All the drivers were certainly concerned and wanted to expand their knowledge. We all wanted to know: How could we be safer inside the car? And why were drivers getting hurt?

In the meantime, we were learning more about internal organs and the fluid they floated in than any of us imagined we would or wanted to know.

The SAFER barrier wall technology and the HANS device were being tested and retested by NASCAR. It wasn't long after Dale's death that tracks all began installing the new barriers. And the HANS head-and-neck device became mandatory. The results prove we are smarter and safer than ever. In the ten years after 2001, NASCAR drivers hit the wall from every angle imaginable and at incredibly high speeds. Not a single one of them died.

Dale always had his own interpretation of the safety rules. At the time of his death, he was one of only a couple of drivers still wearing an open-face helmet. He chose not to use the HANS device. It wasn't that he was cavalier. It's that he wanted to make safety decisions for himself. Dale had done his own research. Based on the walls he had hit and walked away from, he was confident he was safe. That made him kind of old-school, as we all were at the time. We had grown up in an era where we were responsible for our own safety and the interior of our cars. The choices about helmets, seat belts, fireproof gloves—those decisions were the drivers'. Often, we made those decisions based on comfort first and safety second. Racing for six hundred miles, sometimes for more than four hours, on a hot summer Sunday in the South is a tough day's work. You had to be comfortable, we told ourselves, if you were going to win. Back in the day, race-car drivers were macho gladiators. We would figure it out. That was our space. We didn't want anybody else messing around in there.

How funny does that sound? We're talking about 2001 as "back in the day." I mean, we had computers then. It couldn't have been that long ago. But with NASCAR safety, that's how much things have changed. What we know about safety today makes ten years seem like a hundred.

Since then, NASCAR has gotten more and more involved in the details of driver safety. Today, while our input is encouraged, NASCAR makes the final decisions about keeping drivers safe. And that's a good thing. We weren't doing a very good job.

Dale and I had spoken about all of these safety concerns. It was his belief that a driver needed to "ride a crash down," as he put it. He believed, if you were strapped in tightly, a sudden stop would jerk a knot in your neck. That could be dangerous.

His thinking made a lot of sense to me. It reminds you of the SAFER walls. They keep anything from suddenly happening. Dale may have been ahead of his time in how he thought. Tighter belts and stiffer seats were a contrast to his riding-a-crash-down theory.

Did that skepticism cost him his life? That would be hard to say. You couldn't be certain. No one could be. Not only because of how he thought, but also because of the ripped seat-belt discovery. One of Dale's belts had frayed during the crash. Could that be the reason Dale Earnhardt died? There were so many questions being asked. We were all learning about advances in safety technology. For better or worse, we all shared at least some of Dale's attitudes about safety.

I faced the same questions every weekend. All drivers did. The HANS device was something all of us were curious about. Some drivers were already wearing it. Others had tested it and elected not to use it. There were mixed reviews. People liked the way it stabilized the head in an accident but were concerned that it was cumbersome and made it hard to get in and out of the car, which could be a problem. One thing we all liked the sound of was a softer wall. We had all hit concrete enough to know that it hurt. When you took on concrete, ten times out of ten it won. Concrete was undefeated.

I will never forget the first time I hit a SAFER barrier. It was in Miami, 2004, the final race of the NASCAR season. Buffy, Macy, Caitlin, some friends, their kids, and I were going to the Dominican Republic for a few days of fun and sun after a long season. I went down to turn one. Just as I turned into the corner, the right front tire blew out. The instant that happened, I looked up and saw a wall. It looked white and hard. Holy crap, I thought. This is bad. I won't be going on vacation tomorrow.

For twenty-four years, from 1981 to 2004, when I blew a tire, I hit concrete. And that wall looked just like concrete to me.

I gripped my steering wheel, braced my body, gritted my teeth, and thought to myself, Aw, man. This is going to hurt.

But after I hit, it felt like I'd been in nothing more than a pillow fight. I was shocked, and I was thankful. That next day on the beach, as I sipped a fruity drink with frilly umbrellas and fruit on toothpicks, I was thankful for all the people who made that technology part of my world.

I knew I wouldn't be on that beach if it weren't for those people— NASCAR, the engineers who developed the technologies, but most of all my fellow drivers who had paid the ultimate price of plowing into concrete, people who were my friends, and one who was a real close friend of mine, Dale Earnhardt.

But up until the day that Dale died, we didn't get it. Maybe the latest deaths were just a run of bad luck. After all, racing was dangerous. You didn't have to be very bright to figure that out. All you had to do was look around. You were strapped into a steel cage with a fireproof suit on, wearing a helmet. Those should have been some pretty good clues.

We all agree now. The HANS device and the SAFER barrier save lives. But at the time Dale lost his, we were all just looking for answers.

CHAPTER 28

THE FUNERAL

It was Tuesday morning in Mooresville, North Carolina. Those of us inside Dale Earnhardt, Inc. were trying to absorb all that had occurred. We had already decided we were going racing that weekend, and that meant being in Rockingham in four days. I wasn't sure I could do that at a time like this.

Dale Junior, Park, and I were sitting around a long conference-room table at DEI. All the chairs at the table were full—except one. Dale's.

Ty was there. Richie and all the crew chiefs and engineers. We were discussing car setups and race strategies for Rockingham. Our teams hadn't done this before Daytona. Everyone did their own thing going there. This meeting was an attempt to make sure we had our heads in the game and we were as ready as possible.

I sat there and tried to pay attention. But it wasn't happening. I had made it my goal to publicly say all the right things after Sunday's tragedy. But privately, I was all messed up. I was thinking nutty stuff. That day, as I looked around the room, out of the dozen or so people who were in that meeting, I knew most of their names but I only knew a couple of them well.

What were all those other people thinking? I wondered. Did they think Dale's accident was my fault? Were they mad at me? I didn't know.

Everywhere I went, I wondered that. I had been that way for two days. I couldn't get over it. There I sat, looking around. Every now and then, I'd catch a word the engineers and crew chiefs were saying. But that's about it. I looked down at Dale Junior, and he didn't look like he was into the meeting either. He mostly just looked down at the table the whole time. On the other hand, Park and his team seemed focused. They looked like they were into this dumb gathering.

Just down the hall from where our group was discussing Rockingham, Teresa and the other Earnhardt family members had the somber job of figuring out the details of Dale's funeral.

That wouldn't be easy. So many people were flocking to the Mooresville area, there was no simple way to accommodate everyone who wanted to be part of honoring Dale. The best way to achieve that, the family decided, was to hold a small private gathering on Wednesday at St. Mark's Lutheran Church in Mooresville just for the Earnhardt family and a few close friends. That would be followed on Thursday by a larger, invitation-only memorial service at Charlotte's massive Calvary Church, which seats 5,800 people on three levels.

NASCAR put out a statement outlining the plan: "Because it is impossible to accommodate the tremendous outpouring of support to all those who followed Dale, we are unable to open the service to the public. With that in mind, the family has chosen to broadcast the service live on television, enabling fans across the country to share in this service for Dale."

Buffy and I and our family attended both services, showing the Earnhardt family our love.

Wednesday night was a special time for all of us in attendance. Dale's pastor, the Reverend Johnny Cozart, spoke about the Dale that most of those closest to him knew. Not the Intimidator. Not the Man in Black. The quiet Dale. The family Dale. The Dale who had a real spiritual side.

I can tell you Dale didn't walk around publicizing his faith. He didn't talk to people about what was going on inside him.

"But when it came to faith, Dale knew what he believed in," the pastor said. "He believed in the Lord. He sinned. He fell short like all of us do. But he loved Jesus Christ. He had such a positive influence on everyone."

The minister continued. "Whenever I'd visit with him, I'd always leave with a spring in my step."

Dale wasn't churchy in the traditional sense, the pastor said. "He was just a guy who loved people. He was not intimidated by anybody." I guess we all know that, right?

That had touched the minister personally. "I grew up intimidated by certain people. He taught me to be a more assertive pastor and a leader of God's people."

How 'bout Dale? I knew he knew how to make me a better race-car driver. But he also knew how to make the preacher be a better preacher.

Everyone who knew Dale, the minister said, had stories of small kindnesses from him. "One day after church, this lady was out in the parking lot and her car wouldn't start. Dale went out and tried to see what was wrong with it. He raised the hood. He looked around. But he couldn't fix it. 'I'll drive you home,' he told her. 'I'll see that the car is fixed.' He took the lady home and took the car and got it fixed. That's the kind of story I don't think too many ever heard about Dale."

For the memorial service at Calvary Church on Thursday, people packed all the streets nearby. It looked like about forty TV satellite trucks were parked outside the church. Dale was a huge and influential figure. However, Teresa wanted the service to be relatively subdued and brief.

She made sure the inside of the church was beautiful and dignified. Near the pulpit was a white-and-black floral arrangement in the shape of a 3. All the top NASCAR executives were there, as were most all of the race-car drivers, including Sterling Marlin. It was good to see Sterling there. I knew the rough time he'd been experiencing since Dale's crash. Mom and children, along with Teresa, were all seated in the front row.

After an introduction by Pastor Cozart, Motor Racing Outreach chaplain Dale Beaver gave the eulogy. Motor Racing Outreach is NASCAR's traveling church. A lot of the drivers, crew members, and NASCAR officials attend its services along with their families.

As Reverend Beaver began to speak, he described the first day he walked into the Intimidator's hauler to ask the legendary driver to sign a permission slip allowing Dale's daughter Taylor Nicole to go on a youth-group camping trip. "I didn't come into the presence of a racing icon or an intimidating figure," he said. "I came into the presence of a dad."

The minister found a lesson in that for everyone, and he shared it with the congregation. "You and I will one day be ushered into the presence of a very intimidating force," he said. "There's a savior that will take you there."

Randy Owen, lead singer of the group Alabama and a friend of Dale's, stood and shared a beautiful song. His tribute to Dale touched all of us. "Good-bye," Randy sang. "Good-bye till I see you again."

I guess it's been too much fun,
We've shared and we've won.
Yes, the best is yet to come.

Good-bye, good-bye,
Till I see you again.
Good-bye, good-bye,
I'll love and I'll miss you till then.

There were tears in everyone's eyes as we said good-bye to our friend Dale.

When Randy had finished, Teresa made her way to the pulpit to speak to the assembled. It seemed as if she was there to share her thoughts with everyone, but that was simply too much. She clutched her hands to her chest and whispered two barely audible words: "Thank you."

After the funeral and days of tears and sad faces, a group of us who worked at DEI decided it was time to smile. We had all cried enough. We gathered for a good-bye lunch, sending off Dale in our own special way, a way that I know he would have hugely appreciated.

Ty, Richie, me, and all the wives and families celebrated Dale's life. We told stories about the fun times we'd had together, laughing and cherishing the memories.

Like the time in the Bahamas that Ty and I decided we would go jogging, and Dale said he wanted to go with us. Ty and I came out in our running shorts and shoes. When Dale walked up, he had on a big ol' pair of fishing shorts, black socks, and a pair of those shoes you wear on a boat.

"How far you boys want to go?" he asked.

The first quarter mile consisted of two lefts and one right. The right headed you out of the marina and up toward town, which is where Ty and I were planning on running. Dale elected to make three lefts and quickly ran right back to the boat. When Ty and I got back from our run, Dale was sitting on the back of the boat drinking a margarita.

When we walked up all sweaty, Dale said: "I can't run like that unless something's chasing me. But I'll bet you guys can't climb a tree like I can. I can shimmy right up one. Without any spikes either. I'd like to see you two try that."

We laughed that day and said: "You got us there, Dale."

Everyone at lunch thought that story was so Dale. We couldn't stop laughing. We had to explain to the waitress when she walked up that she'd have to excuse us. We had just come from a funeral.

Despite the laughter and my public façade that I was at peace with Dale's death, clearly I wasn't. I mostly felt guilty.

I felt at least partly responsible. Had I not been there, this wouldn't have happened. I know I was just doing what I was told. But whatever, a different Dale was racing his car that day. The Intimidator was being the Defender. He was fighting people off for Dale Junior and me.

Ultimately, being the Defender was why Dale crashed, and I couldn't get that out of my mind.

I took that nagging feeling everywhere with me. Whether I was in the garage area or somewhere signing autographs for fans, I kept wondering: Do they think it's my fault? Or am I the only one thinking that? I couldn't figure it out in my mind, and it was making me crazy.

While I wrestled with these questions internally, the clock kept ticking. I knew I had to get back into that car at Rockingham. Dale's car. Just a week before, climbing into that car felt like heaven to me. Now it was my duty. For the first time in my life I didn't want to be at a racetrack.

I didn't want to be anywhere.

CHAPTER 29

TO ROCKINGHAM

We were going to Rockingham?
          How could we do that?

The answer was because we had to.

Plus, that's what Dale would have expected us to do. We knew that. And Dale would have been extremely clear about his feelings, I'm sure.

"Get your asses to the track, you pansies," he would have said. Or maybe he'd have used some other P-word. You would have definitely gotten his point. "Quit moping around the shop and go racing."

And that's exactly what we did.

It was a tough week. But when the garage opened on Friday morning at Rockingham Speedway, we were there: Dale Junior's bright red Budweiser car, Park's yellow Pennzoil Chevy, and my #15 NAPA car—all three Dale Earnhardt, Inc. teams were at the track and ready to race.

Physically there and ready, at least.

One of our three drivers for sure wasn't able to step up and put behind him what had happened just a few days before and focus on the Rock. That was me. Dale Junior didn't exactly seem one hundred percent either. But all of us understood, I think. It wasn't just our feelings that mattered. We had to be there for others even more.

Our whole team thought it was important for us to share a message with the entire racing community when we got to the Rock. The message was that despite the huge loss we had all just suffered—NASCAR, the competitors, the sport, the fans, all of us—the season would go on. The sport would race forward.

To help us deliver that message, NASCAR organized a press conference for Friday morning prior to the cars hitting the track. When I got out of bed I tried to prepare myself mentally for the day. Not sleeping well was something I'd gotten used to that week, so that wasn't a big problem. But now I had to go to another press conference and talk about the most emotionally challenging day of my life.

I said a prayer, took a deep breath, walked into the room where the media were, and took my seat. It was Dale Junior, Park, and me. We were seated in front of a huge throng of media types, by far the most I'd ever seen at Rockingham. The track is a little off the beaten path in central North Carolina—well, actually, a lot off the beaten path. Coming just a week after Daytona, the Rockingham media coverage usually consisted of the regular NASCAR reporters and the local papers, radio, and TV. That would be about it.

Not this time.

There was so much media in Rockingham, the track officials had to put up a temporary media center. I revived my Monday-after-the-race attitude. This was another opportunity to honor Dale, a man who was inspirational to so many. Dale was an ordinary guy who did extraordinary things. Big E made the American dream seem real to everyone. He was rich and was adored by the masses, yet he was still Dale from Kannapolis. I believed if those who loved him saw me being strong and showing my faith in where Dale was now, that might help them deal with this tragedy.

I started the press conference by saying that we had had an incredibly tough week dealing with the loss of Dale and explaining what he meant to all of us.

"Dale's mom, Teresa, Dale Junior, Kelly, Kerry, Taylor, the team," I said, "my heart goes out to each of you. Despite how painful this is, we're here, ready to race on. Everyone at DEI knows that is what Dale would have expected us to do, and that helps a lot."

I took a long, slow, deep breath. Then I told a bit of a lie.

"Being back at the track is a good thing for us," I went on. "It's a good thing for our crew and our family. When we walk back in the garage area, we're back in our element, doing the things we've done for so long. It will help all of us with the healing process."

That's what I said that morning. It was the right thing to say. But it wasn't exactly the truth for me personally. I was putting up a good front. Being there hurt. I wasn't into it. As soon as I stopped talking, I knew there would be questions I didn't want to answer, about thoughts I just wasn't prepared to share. And I was right. It began with the first question.

"Can you talk about your emotions last Sunday?" one of the reporters asked. "You finally win, only to find out about Dale's death?"

I knew that was coming. I also knew what I was going to say.

"The short answer is no," I said. "I can't talk about that. Not this week. Maybe after we get through this weekend, we can talk about how I feel. But this week, I don't want to do that. Let this be a week that we just talk about Dale and what he's meant to all of us. Next week, or someday, we can talk about all that other emotional stuff." I had no idea how far out that someday might be. Maybe it would be a book one day.

"This week, let's talk about fun things," I went on. "Like one of the memories that I'll always cherish is me, these two"—Dale Junior and Park—"and Dale Earnhardt running 1-2-3-4 in the Daytona 500. For him to be able to see that and know his guys were right up there with him leading the race, he had to think that was the coolest thing in the whole world. I know there is a picture of all of us up there, and I want one. Because I can see Dale grinning now. What a special memory for the three of us that will always be."

As the questions went to Park and Junior, I was thinking about what an overwhelming week it had been. It was just the previous Friday that Dale had given me all that direction about how we were going to win the 500. And when the checkered flag fell over me at Daytona—after the way Dale had helped me, with me having no idea he was hurt there in turn four—for a little bit there in Victory Lane, I wanted to tell the world, "Hey, y'all. I could win the championship this year. I mean, why not? I got everything I need to do it." That's where Dale had me.

I was so focused, I believed I could do anything. He had built my confidence to a height it had never reached before.

That's exactly where I was mentally. It was all the way to the top. In my mind, confidence has to be based on reality. You can't just make stuff up. And I wasn't making any of it up.

Before Daytona, I'd had that great test in Rockingham. When that test ended, I believed I could win at the Rock too. I was that fast. There was no way things could have been any better in my world. There was a new guy in charge of my career, and his name was Dale. Together, we had done something I had never been able to do by myself—win when it counted.

The thoughts went rushing through my head.

Where to next? I wondered. Tell me how we're gonna win Rockingham, Dale! I know you know how! I've seen you do it before!

Yet here I was. Instead of showing up at Rockingham thinking about a championship, I was there to do a press conference about our lost leader, my lost friend. I was there to explain that although Dale was gone, we were going to keep racing because that's what he would have expected us to do.

I was there doing the right things—saying the right things—because of Dale and for Dale's fans. I wasn't there because I wanted to be. I was there because I needed to be. There were things I wanted people to hear about Dale from me. Stories like the one Reverend Cozart had told about Dale's fixing that lady's car and about Dale's faith. I needed to tell stories about Dale that few had ever heard before. I needed for people to know the Dale that I knew.

My favorite was the story of Dale coming to see my mom after Dad died. People who didn't know better might have thought the driver they called the Intimidator would be headed straight down instead of up. "That's why they call him the Man in Black," you'd hear people say. "He'll straighten 'em out down there. Before you know it, he'll be running that place."

Actually, we called him the Man in Black because that was the color of his car.

But most didn't know Dale. They weren't sitting at Mom's house when Dale came over to hug her the day after my dad died. They didn't see him hold her hand and tell her how much my daddy meant to him and how special she and Dad were for putting up with Darrell and me all those years. Momma thought that was funny. She also thought it was incredibly sweet of Dale to drive all the way to Sherrills Ford to comfort her.

As the press conference continued, another question was directed at me. I didn't exactly hear it because I was thinking about Dale. Instead of answering the question—whatever it was—I wanted people to hear a

Bible verse that had helped me through the week. The verse came from 1 Corinthians 15. I said it the way I had always heard it. "In the twinkling of an eye, you are in the presence of the Lord when you die, if you believe," I told them.

It means you can simply close your eyes right before you die and say, "Forgive me, Lord, I'm a sinner,"and go straight to heaven.

I could picture in my mind Dale getting turned toward the outside wall that day and looking up at it, and saying, "Here I come, Lord. Forgive me and make some room for me." And then probably asking, "Where's my dad and Neil?" and thinking, "I'll bet ol' Leroy is pretty happy up here right now."

I believe that is what happened on February 18, 2001. Believing it allowed me to keep on living, to deal with the guilt, and to keep my head up. I believe we're only here for a short while but are up in heaven for eternity. Eternity is a long time, from what I hear.

In the days and years since then I have had many people come up to me and say, "Your words at that press conference enlightened me. Thank you for your perspective." People heard about a different side of Dale, and it brought them comfort.

What I wanted to say turned out to be what a lot of people needed to hear. I was proud of that. I delivered the message I had come to deliver. I didn't lose it or break down. I said it just like I wanted to. I maintained my calm and composure. I said what was in my heart. I was holding myself together better than I thought I would.

I knew the media would have more questions for me going forward. But that press conference was the last official piece of business for me concerning what had happened at Daytona. I accomplished what I'd set out to do. I had helped people all over who were hurting to find a bit of peace.

I just wished it had helped me. I still had lots of haunting feelings that week that I needed to get over. And I needed to get over them quickly. Dealing with guilt, self-pity, and anger had led to five straight pretty much sleepless nights.

The press conference was behind me and practice was ahead.

Oh, great. Practice. What I needed was a nap.

I had no time for that. Sleepy or not, the reason I was in Rockingham was to race. I had to switch my attention to my car.

. . . .

The track had always been where I wanted to be, where I was the happiest. However, that week, just five days since Daytona, this was not the case.

I'm not proud to say it, but mentally I wasn't there. I tried to talk myself into it before getting in the car: "You've run well here before, Mike. Remember the test in January? You were fast. Your laps were better than both your teammates'. Think about that!"

Plus, I was still driving for Dale Earnhardt, Inc.

"What's your record on this team, Mike?" I asked myself. "That's right. A perfect one for one, undefeated. Let's go get that NAPA car, tune it up, and do it again on Sunday."

Sounds like I did a pretty good job of getting myself ready to go, right?

Yep. Too good.

When practice started, I was fast. I went straight to the top of the speed charts. My car felt great, and I was hauling. After a couple of laps I was back at the garage, and Dale Junior came over. He leaned in with a big smile on his face and said, "Man! Looks good seeing you up near the top. You might know how to drive after all."

Getting Dale Junior's approval was important to me. Us being able to laugh and joke at the track as teammates was so cool. Heck, we didn't even do that in Daytona the week before.

But just when I really started feeling good about where I was and what I was doing, I ruined it. Flat screwed up. Coming off turn four late in practice, I lost control of my car and spun into the outside wall. Hard. My car was destroyed, along with my positive attitude and my confidence.

What Dale Junior had said kept replaying in my head. "You might know how to drive after all." After I wrecked, I'm sure he was thinking, ". . . or not."

I'd gotten all caught up in the moment. The positive talk about how fast I was made me push too hard. My dad would have said, "Looks like you can't stand prosperity, son." And he would have been right.

After my Daytona win and my early speed at Rockingham, people were maybe starting to believe in me like Dale had. I messed it all up by making a stupid mistake.

I was crushed. Just prior to that crash was the last time I felt good about racing for a long while. We unloaded our backup car and qualified seventh. I went on to finish thirteenth. I looked at the whole weekend as a wasted opportunity. Instead of having a chance to win, I finished thirteenth. Dale Junior's weekend sucked too. He had a crash early in the race. I'm sure he was happy to get out of Rockingham, as was I.

Remember me saying Steve Park and his team seemed more focused preparing for Rockingham? Well, they were. In a dramatic finish, Steve held off Bobby Labonte and won. How about that for Dale Earnhardt, Inc.? Our team was back in Victory Lane again. Steve had stepped up and given the whole organization just what it needed.

Thanks to Steve and his team, the healing could continue, as did Dale's winning tradition.

CHAPTER 30

DAYTONA RETURN

You ever just know something? You see it. You feel it. You can't prove it exactly. But you just know it's true.

Happens to me all the time. One time was when I showed up at Daytona in 2001 with Dale, dragging all those losses behind me. That man had me convinced I could win. I believed him, and he was right. The next time I felt something like that was a few months later, in early June, when it was almost time to return to the beach. I was at Pocono or Michigan or wherever it was, someplace I didn't want to be, and I was struggling. The season I'd dreamed of my whole life had turned into a nightmare after the first race. Such an unbelievable win—and at the same time, an unimaginable loss. That contradiction had me stumbling through a life I didn't want to be living, constantly reminded of a day I wanted desperately to forget.

That day in February was the last time I had smiled at the track. That was before I knew about Dale. I'd had a little hope down at Rockingham a week later, when my car was fast and Dale Junior and I were joking about my performance. But then I wiped out and that was the end of that and the beginning of week after week of racing disappointment.

Nothing went right. Yet every week there I was, back at another track, doing what I was supposed to do. I didn't really feel like it was me doing it. I felt like I was just going through the motions, taking one meaningless green flag after another. But all that was going to change, and it was about time. I woke up that June morning and I felt different. I felt inspired again, for some reason. And I liked it. I must have had a dream, I don't know. But the first words out of my mouth that morning were "Daytona's coming up, Buff—and when we're there, it's gonna be game on. That place owes us, baby. It broke our hearts and derailed our lives. And I'm gonna go there and make things right."

I could tell Buffy liked what she was hearing. I asked her, "Can you imagine how mad Dale is?"

I was wandering around all lost, looking for someone else to fix my problems? Unacceptable. Dale would never have put up with that. I wasn't going to either. I was being a quitter, and I ain't no quitter. Quitters don't lose four hundred and sixty-two races in a row. They don't get the chance. I was going to do what Dale had expected of me. I could hear him saying, "Put your heart in your car. Go down there and do what I hired you for, you P-word."

Yes, sir, boss!

Our Daytona return was still a couple of weeks away, and what a return it would be.

Saturday night under the lights, Fourth of July, Independence Day weekend. This would be a fireworks show, NASCAR-style. I was going south with an attitude. Nobody had heard much from Mikey since the last time we were down there. But they'd be hearing from me soon.

When I was a kid, they called the July race at Daytona the Firecracker 400. Now it's the Coke Zero 400. It has always been one of my favorite races of the year. It's our chance to celebrate America's independence. We racing people always do our best celebrating at the track.

With each day that passed, I thought about Daytona and became more and more energized. My heart rate rose. I wanted revenge.

I loved that feeling. I had missed it. The fire was back.

When we got to Daytona, I was more than ready to get my season on track. My mission started with the first lap of practice. I was one with my car. I felt every bump on the track. Every adjustment on the car made perfect sense to me. It was as if I knew how the car was going to react before it reacted.

I had been lost for months without any focus or direction. My race team minus Dale wasn't helping me much either. He was going to be my team leader, and he was gone. Scott, who'd started the year as my crew chief, wasn't at DEI anymore. We replaced him with one interim guy and then another. By the time July rolled around, I didn't even have a crew chief.

But I didn't care about that detail at Daytona. I would take over there. In my mind, no one was better than me on that track.

I thought about every move I had ever made at Daytona, every move that had ever worked for me. How I set people up. Where I made most of my passes. I planned how and when I would use those moves—and win. My attitude was, "I'm better than the competition. They will see." I'm not sure I know exactly what "being in the zone" means. But I do know I was somewhere close to that zone.

Despite it being a night race, my day started early that Saturday. I had an eight A.M. tee time at the LPGA golf course in Daytona with fellow racer and Daytona winner Dale Jarrett. His brother, Glenn, and Ty Norris completed the foursome. I liken this golf game to my February pre-race sit-down on the bumper of my truck, the counseling session I'd given myself. That session was about me relaxing, taking my time, and letting the race come to me. Golf that morning was the same thing. I even shot a birdie.

I knew that night I'd have two teammates out on the track with me. But you need all the help you can get. I thought maybe I could work my charm with Jarrett on the golf course so if he had a choice of who to draft with that night, he would pick me instead of some other dude. I was working every possible angle. Jarrett commented about how fast my car had been in practice all week. I loved hearing that again. Hadn't heard that since February.

I was feeling like Confident Mike again. I liked the way this day was shaping up: some golf, a quick nap, a little dinner—and then I'd be off to do what I'd come to Daytona for. I hadn't been sad for one moment leading up to my Daytona return. Just focused. I had successfully blocked out all the emotions that were associated with the last time I was there. I was ready—and a little mad.

Then it was time to head out for driver introductions. Buffy and I started the walk. That took us by where Dale's bus had always been parked. I'd walked by that spot about a hundred times that week. But this time it really hit me. For the first time that weekend, I felt the sadness. There wasn't a bus there. The spot was empty. This was the place where he told me in February how we were going to win. As Buffy and I walked by, I could almost see him sticking his head out that door and yelling over to me. Tears began running down my cheeks. Damn, I didn't want to do that. I didn't say a word. Buffy didn't either. There weren't any words to say. She just wiped the tears away, and we kept walking, heading to Pit Road.

As the introductions began, the crowd was just amazing. As big as ever, and more enthusiastic than I'd seen. When Dale Junior and I got introduced, the cheers were the loudest I'd heard. We were definitely the crowd favorites. It felt so good to know the fans were supporting us like that. But I knew it wasn't only us they were cheering for. They were also cheering for Dale.

The only way to respond to that was to go win. When the green flag flew, I could tell my car was good. I was competitive. Dale Junior's car was better though. He was borderline dominant.

It was pretty much your typical restrictor-plate race—tons of action, lots of passing, and a couple of wrecks. As the laps wound down, just like in February, Junior and I had gotten ourselves in a position to win. One last pit stop was all that was left. If I was going to accomplish what I had come to Daytona for, it looked like I would have to beat Dale Junior to do it. Every time I looked up, his bad #8 car was racing right at the front.

I was ready to charge. A little too ready, I guess. And I made a mistake. I hate how I keep doing that, damn it!

"Pit," came the call over the radio. And I hit Pit Road.

We needed a good pit stop if I was going to win. Passing was way more difficult than it had been in February. In an effort to make the races safer, NASCAR had changed the rules after the Daytona 500. Instead of the radical aerodynamic package we ran in February, we were running under more traditional rules. So track position was very important, and I wanted to help my crew all I could.

I dove hard into my pit stall. I knew I needed to get in there fast. But I was going too fast. When I hit the brakes, they locked up. I slid right through my pit. When I came to a stop, I was way past my crew. Lucky for me there wasn't a car in the stall ahead of me, or I would have hit it. Even worse, I would probably have hit the crew guys too. Since that stall was empty and I didn't hit anything or anyone, I just backed up, got my tires and gas, and returned to the track. I was thankful that I had the chance to return to the track and get back all those spots I'd lost.

But, man, I was mad at myself.

Instead of helping my crew gain a couple or three spots, my mistake cost us about twenty. And there wasn't a worse time to do it. There weren't many laps to go, fewer than ten, and I was stuck back in the pack.

So I had to lean on that Friday morning lesson Dale had taught me when we were here back in February: Don't worry about yesterday. I couldn't worry about that pit stop. There was no time for that. I had to go get another win. That's what I'd come to Daytona to do.

I was down. But I wasn't out. There was enough time. I knew it would take some very aggressive driving and some great moves. But I knew how to make those moves. I started making them as soon as the green flag waved, and I was right. What I was doing was working.

High. Low. Middle. Three-wide, you name it. I was on it. From twentieth to the front.

While I was fighting my way through traffic with just a few laps to go, Dale Junior grabbed the lead. With two to go, I'd raced my way to third. By the time we came back for the white flag, with another great pass I had done it: I was in the second spot. The only car ahead of me was Dale Junior.

He was next.

"Go get him, Mike," I was telling myself. "You're gonna win this race. You're gonna win at Daytona again."

As we raced off turn two for the last time, Junior was a sitting duck. I had a huge run on him. I was gaining fast, and Elliott Sadler in the Wood Brothers car was locked on my bumper and pushing hard.

I'm going to do it, I thought. I got the run to pass him with, and I know it. He's done.

The five seconds that it took from the time I realized I could pass him to when I needed to pull out and make the move—it seemed like forever. For five seconds, time stood still. I was seeing it all in slow motion. And I thought about so many different things.

I thought about Dale. I thought about how much I missed him. I thought about how badly the last five months had hurt me. I thought about how tough it was for Buffy, having to live with my miserable butt.

I thought how it must have been for Junior—heck, for all of Dale's family—living with so much pain.

And the more I thought about it, the farther I tried to shove that gas pedal through the floorboard: all the anger, sorrow, disappointment, and frustration welling up and me trying to squeeze it all out with my right foot. I was gritting my teeth and almost in tears, I was so mad. Five months of denial—five months of feelings I had suppressed—came gushing out of me in those five seconds.

"Put him away, Mike!" I told myself. "No one's ever needed a win worse than you do now. It's right there for the taking!"

I was thinking all of that, and his car was getting bigger and bigger in my windshield. I knew this win was mine.

All the struggles of this season will be over, I thought, as soon as I make this pass. And I was on my way to doing it.

Just as I drafted up on Junior's bumper and went to pull out to make the pass, something happened that I can't explain. Instead of whipping out and going around, I just held the wheel straight and rolled right in behind him.

What?

What just happened? I wondered. Why didn't I pass him? I had him. Who's driving my car here?

Who knows?

Was it divine intervention? Maybe it was. I know I wasn't in charge. Maybe Big E was.

Could he have steered my car right in behind Junior's? That's where I ended up and certainly not where I planned to be.

I was pushing Dale Junior to the checkered flag, just like he had done for me back in February. Dale told Junior to push me then. Did he just tell me to push Junior?

I thought that winning was what I had to do to get my Daytona revenge. But as we drove under the checkered flag one-two, I've never felt more like a winner in my life.

Now, this is complicated because no race-car driver likes losing. But no race-car driver, probably no human being, had ever been through the emotions that I had the last time I was in Daytona. There was no standard for the feelings I was dealing with: the greatest triumph of my life followed immediately by such a devastating tragedy.

I am so glad I made that decision. Or whoever made it. Crossing the finish line one-two—with me being the two guy—was absolutely perfect. I was ecstatic, and so were the fans.

After the race was over, the cheers were so loud I could hear them over my engine. I hadn't ever heard anything louder than my engine before. But that night in Daytona, the fans were that loud.

When Dale Junior completed his victory lap, he pulled onto the infield grass at the start-finish line and began spinning his car around, waving his arm in the air. The crowd was going nuts. I needed to be part of that.

So I pulled my car onto the grass beside Junior's when he stopped spinning. As I pulled up, Junior ran over and leaned inside my car. "Can you believe this shit?" he said. "That was awesome. Listen to those people."

And he was right. It was awesome.

The capacity crowd continued to cheer. Loudly. A hundred and fifty thousand people, maybe more, were there when the green flag was thrown. After the checkered, all of them had gotten up from their seats. But not a one of them had left. They were standing, cheering, screaming, and celebrating our amazing finish.

And they were celebrating the life of Dale Earnhardt.

This ain't wrestling. You can't script the moments like this in real sports. This was one of those moments, a time when a sporting event can make everything seem right. There are times when sports can be better medicine than any doctor can provide.

When Dale Junior walked away from my car, I quickly climbed out and jumped up on the roof to salute the fans. "Thank y'all," I yelled. "And thank you, Dale. I'm glad you woke me up before we got here."

That angry man driving down the back straightaway a few minutes ago? He didn't exist anymore.

Our finish exorcised him.

The angry man who had given up on his season, his sport, something he had been so passionate about his whole life—that man was gone too. And back was my love for Daytona.

Dale Junior then jumped on top of my car with me. He grabbed me and we hugged each other really hard. I think we were both getting the hug we had missed after the 500, a hug we each had been needing for five months now. It was just us hugging. But I could feel Dale with us too.

What a moment! This was why I couldn't wait to get back to Daytona.

The record books will always show Dale Junior won that night. But I know that result gave me more satisfaction than any mark in the win column ever could.

While we were saluting the crowd on top of my car, our entire team ran out to celebrate with us and the fans. Before he climbed off my car, Junior looked at me and said: "I love you, man."

"I love you too, Bro," I said.

Then he turned to his team and dove off my car, headfirst right into the middle of them. They caught him perfectly. He was crowd-surfing like he was at a Phish concert.

I thought that looked like so much fun, I wanted a Phish dive too. But my team started waving their arms frantically.

"No, no, no," they shouted. "Don't jump. You're kinda big, dude. Plus you're too old to be crowd-surfing, anyway."

I guess they thought I was Phished out.

CHAPTER 31

HE'S BACK

Oh, what a night!
That's a song from the Sixties, by the way. Frankie Valli sings about the year I was born.

When I finally got to bed that Saturday, I was feeling so content, relishing my return to Daytona and the unexpected last-minute decision I had made. I'd thought I had to win the race that night, but I was wrong. I got everything I needed by finishing second. It couldn't have been more triumphant. The story of our return to Daytona had a storybook ending. I did the right thing for the right reasons and pushed Dale Junior home. Together, we had done something special for the fans. Dale Junior and I got to celebrate our one-two finish. Us getting to celebrate at Daytona healed a lot of people's wounds.

I wanted this feeling to last forever. And I assumed that it would. Finally, I figured, I could live normally. The feelings that had haunted me the past five months—the guilt, the sadness, the sorrow—they'd be history. I had left them on the back straightaway that special night in Daytona when I tried to push my gas pedal through the floor and successfully pushed Dale Junior to victory.

Or had I?

As I was sleeping Saturday night, all those haunting feelings must have climbed into bed with me. When I woke up Sunday morning, I stretched, looked around, and recognized them immediately: "What are y'all doin' here? Didn't I get rid of you last night?"

I wasn't alarmed at first. In my simple brain, I just figured, well, maybe it would take a few days to shake these suckers off. After all, I'd been down in the dumps for five months. This might be a little harder to escape from than I anticipated. Losing those feelings might take more than one special night at the track. I was happy we had a trip to the islands planned for that afternoon. I felt certain Customs wouldn't allow these complexities into the Bahamas when we got there that morning.

We got up early. We packed Macy's floaties. We gathered up our swimsuits. And we boarded our plane to Nassau. We were going to meet Teresa there and spend some time with her on *Sunday Money,* her and Dale's boat. This was our first trip back to the Bahamas without Dale.

When we'd planned the vacation a few months earlier, Buffy and I had wondered: Would it feel weird being down there without him? We loved Boat Dale. He was so relaxed, so casual. You could tell he was at total peace.

I explained to Buff it wouldn't be much different for me. It was something I'd been dealing with every weekend—being somewhere Dale was supposed to be and he wasn't.

Our attitude was: "It'll seem like old times." Captain Terry and the crew on the boat always made us feel special when we were aboard. Plus, we'd hardly seen Teresa since February, so it would be fun to catch up with her and hang out.

And what nice timing this was. Those people were going to be happy to see me. Dale Junior and I had presented a gift to NASCAR fans everywhere. And I still couldn't get over how the ones in Daytona reacted, how loud their screaming was. I knew Teresa and all the folks down in the Bahamas were doing the same thing that night. Sitting on the boat, watching the race on TV, and cheering.

This was the perfect little trip for us, going to the Bahamas, staying on the boat that we loved so much, and getting to see Teresa and a bunch of other NASCAR folks. When we got there, the reception was just as warm as I thought it would be. There were smiles everywhere. And even though technically it might have been a little before noon that Sunday morning, we justified the champagne we were drinking by saying we were on island time. We were toasting Dale Junior's and my special one-two finish. The whole Jimmy Buffett "It's Five O'Clock Somewhere" adage was all the cover we needed.

Can you imagine the stark contrast between the day after this Daytona race and the one in February? The first one hurt so bad. This one felt so good. I knew between the boat and the champagne, those feelings that got in bed with me the night before wouldn't be bugging me in the Bahamas.

After a perfect day on the boat, swimming with the kids and hanging with the adults, Buff and I lay down that night. And guess who joined us?

I suppose there would be no escaping my demons. I realized right there, lying in the Bahamas, that the pain of what happened in February would always be a part of who I was.

Our trip was brief. We had to be in Chicago for the next weekend's race. That Wednesday evening, we headed home just three days after we arrived. When we got back to North Carolina, I couldn't stand it anymore. I had to tell Buffy that those feelings that had been living with me for the past five months were taking up permanent residence. Those feelings were going to be there, no matter what happened at the track or how many vacations we took. I was just going to have to live with them.

"I don't want to talk about it," I told her that night. "I don't want you counseling me. I'm just going to live with it and deal with it on my own."

She was sad to hear me say that. That wasn't the Mike she married. But she seemed to resign herself to thinking that's just how it was going to be.

Despite my unwillingness to deal with the pain of Dale's death, I was done ignoring my career. The attitude I took to Daytona with me, the drive-with-your-heart guidance Dale would have given me—I was going to take that everywhere.

I had a plan, which was to go to DEI and tell Ty and Richie I was tired of what had gone on up until Daytona. I wanted some changes. "I want a crew chief," I said. "I want someone to be in charge of my team like Park and Dale Junior have. And boys, if we get the right guy, I promise you I will win DEI some races."

I made it clear. I wanted Ty and Richie both to know. They were now dealing with an inspired Mike. I wasn't messing around.

"I'm not being treated fairly," I said. "Give me a guy. Put someone in charge of my team, somebody who can take my car, my crew, and put them on his back. We have been running my team this year with people who seem like they couldn't care less. I have one crew chief one week and another the next. Heck, I don't even have a crew chief now. There's definitely no leader on my team. That's not fair."

They supported me, and the search for my guy began.

It took a while, but we found that guy. In late September, Richard "Slugger" Labbe joined DEI as my crew chief. Slugger's presence did just what I hoped it would. He cared as much as I did. He was just who I needed just when I needed him. He was passionate about building my cars. He wanted to make every detail perfect.

I told Richie and Ty to get someone like Slugger because that's something Dale would have done. When Slugger showed up, I started winning. In 2002, I won my qualifying race for the 500. When we returned in July, we won the 400. And in February 2003, I won my second Daytona 500.

How 'bout that? I finally did something my brother hadn't.

Mikey: Two Daytona 500 wins.
DW: One.

That's something I know Dale Earnhardt would have been proud of, those Daytona 500 trophies and the success we were enjoying at Daytona in general. In seven straight Daytona races, beginning with the 500 in 2001, my finishes were unprecedented.

2001 Daytona 500: First
2001 Coke Zero 400: Second
2002 Daytona 500 qualifying race: First
2002 Daytona 500: Fifth
2002 Coke Zero 400: First
2003 Daytona 500 qualifying race: Second
2003 Daytona 500: First

Because of the success I had racing at DEI, I was building credibility within NASCAR. More sponsors wanted to be on my car. More fans wanted my autograph.

What a ride I'd had at DEI! Five seasons of ups and downs that changed my life. Five years absorbing the triumph and tragedy that arrived my first day on the job. Those were the most important five years of my life, as I became a winner and learned to deal with losses too. The whole time I was there, I was emotionally all over the place.

Dale's team without Dale was definitely not the same, and by the middle of 2005, I could tell the time had come for me to go. I felt sad about that, although no one at DEI seemed too broken up over my departure. I didn't expect a lot of thanks-Mike-you've-been-a-good-partner-for-DEI, and I didn't get any. I don't think anyone even said good-bye. All the excitement and enthusiasm I'd experienced when Dale called me about driving for him—that was gone.

Because of my success with DEI I had a lot of options to consider.

Various possibilities were being floated. But the one that sounded most interesting to me came from Toyota. Just as I was leaving DEI, Toyota executives announced they were going into NASCAR Sprint Cup racing. They wanted to be up and racing in time for the 2007 season. One of the guys they wanted to go racing with was me.

Toyota wanted me to be a Cup team owner. That was a huge honor. In addition to my Cup performances, Toyota had also noticed my Busch team and the success we were having. The reason I even had a Busch team was because my sponsor, Aaron's, believed in me. Ken Butler, the main man at the Atlanta-based lease-to-own company, made us a key part of his marketing plan in 2000. We'd grown together ever since. Toyota and Aaron's both loved the fact that we were building our Busch cars behind my house. They thought, "If he can build such fast cars behind his house, just imagine what he could do with some of our resources."

When Toyota presented their Cup lineup for 2007, of the seven cars they were going to put on the track, Michael Waltrip Racing would field three of them. That announcement got everyone's attention. For years, foreign manufacturers hadn't been permitted. So Toyota had had a few barriers they needed to break down. They wanted the fans to accept them into NASCAR.

So who better to spread the word of Toyota coming to Cup than a couple of Waltrips? DW and I both believed in Toyota joining NASCAR, and we wanted to tell the world about it. The two of us began meeting folks all over the country who were making a living building and selling Toyota cars and trucks. A couple of new plants had just been built in our neck of the woods, Kentucky and Tennessee, and were providing many jobs in those areas. Darrell and I made TV and radio commercials and appearances all over, welcoming Toyota to NASCAR. At the same time, my Michael Waltrip Racing team was busy building our NASCAR Toyota Camrys.

The guys in the shop behind my house were joined by other guys so we could build more cars. We also needed somewhere to put all this stuff. We were officially out of room in the little Busch shop in Sherrills Ford. So the search for a new home for Michael Waltrip Racing was under way.

We found a vacant movie theater and an indoor skating rink located next to each other in Cornelius, North Carolina, and turned them into a state-of-the-art, fan-friendly racing facility. My vision was to do two things at once at our shop: build cars that could win races, and entertain the race fans who loved visiting the shops.

When Dale first built the Garage-Mahal, people would come from all over the world to see Dale Earnhardt, Inc. They wanted to check out where Dale built his cars. His race shop was nothing near ordinary. It was the most modern shop in NASCAR, the first one that the fans wanted to see.

I wanted to have a shop like Dale's.

I wanted to have a team like Dale's.

Heck, I wanted to win championships like Dale had.

And that was my goal. Not only to produce the results Dale Earnhardt did, but also to run the team like Dale did. I loved walking through DEI by Dale's side. You could tell that everybody who worked there was into building his cars. Their attitude was, "These are Dale Earnhardt's cars. We gotta make them better than everybody else's. That's what Dale expects." And that's what they did. Can you believe my Daytona results? You have to have fast cars to accomplish all that at Daytona. In addition to my wins, Dale Junior won there too. He took the Daytona 500 in 2004, giving Dale's team three out of the four 500 wins from 2001 to 2004.

Those guys knew Dale didn't have to have a team. He wanted to have a team. He had all kinds of money. He had a yacht. He could just spend the weekends goofing off down in the Bahamas. But he loved racing, and he was competitive. So he wanted to build the best race team in NASCAR.

That became my goal too.

I was just like Dale in that way. I wanted to walk through Michael Waltrip Racing and have my guys say, "These are Michael's cars. He's all in. He loves this sport. We gotta make his cars better than anybody else's."

And that's how it was in Sherrills Ford. My little hobby team was just a bunch of guys having fun. But now with the commitment to go Cup racing, we had to grow, just like Dale's team had done over the years. But I needed my small group of guys behind my house to buy into what I was wanting to do. Bobby, Troy, Chris, Glen, Ray-Ray, and David were my main guys. I explained to them that if we were going Cup racing, action was going to have to pick up. In less than a year, we had to be in Daytona with our three-car Cup team, ready to race. From a small Busch team out in the country to a full-time three-car Cup operation was a Herculean task. But my boys all said they were in. We could do it. I believed in them, and those six guys are still with me today.

I also had to beef up my management team. Ty Norris from the old DEI days joined me early on. Ty knew Dale's management style better than anyone. He and Dale ran DEI side by side. I shared with Ty my vision of how Michael Waltrip Racing and Toyota would work together. Ty and I made a plan and then began recruiting team members— everyone from front-office types to truck drivers.

Ty and I were involved in every aspect of building our racing organization. Landing sponsors. Hiring a bunch of people, some of whom came over from DEI and are still with us today. We also had to oversee. construction of our shop. And that was no small task. It was 140,000 square feet of overseeing.

It was important that we understood our relationship with Toyota, how much help they could offer us to ensure we were building our team properly. Toyota Racing Development, TRD, had all the resources to help us build our team but very little experience in NASCAR. Ty and I were about the opposite of TRD. We had been part of winning organizations in NASCAR. But if you looked around our shop in Sherrills Ford, you would say our resources were limited at best.

We were smart enough to realize we had a lot to do and we couldn't do it alone. We needed plenty of help to get from Sherrills Ford to Daytona in a year. The first stop on the way was our newly completed shop in Cornelius. As we prepared for the upcoming season, we leaned heavily on the Toyota people, whose way of conducting business was quite different from what we were used to. Back behind my house, we didn't have too many official meetings. The ones we did have were held down at the barbecue joint where we liked to have lunch. Generally, we could figure out any issue we had over a pulled-pork sandwich. You know what sounds dirty but it ain't? Pulled pork. Jokes like that set the tone for those meetings.

But now we were attending meetings that were much different. We had written agendas. We had PowerPoints. We assigned responsibilities. There was even a girl there taking the minutes. Where did she come from? We even had meetings about upcoming meetings. My stupid jokes didn't seem so appropriate in these meetings. A typical day in early 2006 would start at seven A.M. with—yep, you guessed it—a team meeting. All the managers would get together and outline that day's car-building process. What we were building, what TRD was working on, and how the two would come together. Then by nine we were in a travel meeting. Where were we going and how were we getting there? At one of those meetings, a decision was made that we needed three aircraft to transport our teams to the races and testing that we needed to do to ensure we were competitive.

Three airplanes sounded pretty expensive. Then we had to add on some pilots. And some guys to make sure the maintenance got done. Oh, yeah, and then one more thing. We needed a hangar. We couldn't just let 'em sit outside. And then when it was about time to go, we said, "Oh, shoot. We need some flight attendants."

That was quite an expensive meeting.

The top teams in NASCAR were all established operations. Those owners had had twenty-five-plus years to figure out how to race their cars, a twenty-five-plus-year head start on Michael Waltrip Racing. That also meant twenty-five-plus years of acquiring all the equipment needed to race. Those owners had grown their teams with the sport. The sport was all grown, and we had one year to catch up.

I bet the expense of buying all I had to buy in one year would have gotten those owners' attention—and they were rich. They were old too. Well, let's call them more experienced. They knew how to run a business. I wasn't so good at that yet. There was this word that kept coming up, no matter what meeting I was in. It didn't really make much sense to me. But it must have been important.

That aggravating word? Budget.

Buffy and I had never really operated on one of those.

My philosophy was simple. If Mr. Hendrick or Mr. Penske had a piece of equipment that made their cars faster, then we had to have one too. I had told NAPA, Aaron's, all our sponsors, that we were going to win. If those other teams had more stuff than what we had, how were we going to beat them? That wouldn't be a fair fight.

For a while I was undefeated in those meetings. Airplanes, gotta have, get 'em, check. Shock dynos, chassis pull-down machines, CNC equipment—check, check, check.

We don't have the money yet? Simple. Just like I used to tell Mom. Write a check. That's about how mature I was. And we wrote checks. Lots of them. We had to. We weren't just going to race. We were going to win. I could not wait for the 2007 season to begin.

CHAPTER 32

GOING FORWARD

You are never really ready to go to the races, I have learned. It's just time to go.

And that's what time it was. February 2007. I was finishing up a few last-minute details at the shop before heading to the airport. On my way out of the shop that night, I met a guy making a late delivery.

"What do you have there, bud?" I asked.

"It's your copy machine, Mister Waltrip," he said.

"Cool. We need one of those."

As I drove toward the airport that night, the late delivery of my new copy machine started bothering me. I was thinking, "Shouldn't we already have one of those? What else don't we have? And who's supposed to be in charge of getting it? Is it me?"

I mean, seriously. We just got our copy machine! That handy device just showed up? How did we make it this far without one of those? All the top organizations had probably had their copy machines for twenty-five years. It was about a half hour's drive to the Statesville airport, where we kept our airplanes, and that dumb piece of office equipment had me all torn up the whole way.

You have to understand. We were undefeated. We hadn't lost a race yet. There was so much positive talk around the NASCAR world about what we were building. I'd never heard so many things said about me. But the time to talk was about over. We were one plane ride away from the whole world seeing what we had. I was really nervous about that. I couldn't handle going to Daytona and being embarrassed. In typical

Mikey fashion, I had gone all in. No one in the history of NASCAR had ever started a new team with a new manufacturer and three cars. Most were just one-car teams at the beginning.

Was that a good idea? A little late to wonder that now.

I had bet the farm that we could succeed. Literally. My lovely hundred-acre farm out in Sherrills Ford. What happened next made that a bad bet.

It was qualifying day, and I was up early, eagerly anticipating my team's official NASCAR debut. When the cars hit the track in Daytona, race fans everywhere wanted to see how Toyota would stack up in NASCAR against Ford, Chevy, and Dodge. People were also eager to see how Michael Waltrip Racing would fare. Our new team was big news in Daytona. I was proud of what we had built. I was happy that all three cars had performed well in pre-qualifying practice. I was also happy because I was in Daytona again. But this time I felt different being there, more like a proud new father—except this father was doting over three cars, not three babies.

All cars must pass NASCAR's technical inspection prior to getting onto the track to qualify. This was a routine that NASCAR teams go through before every race. It's usually just that, routine.

So when the phone rang that morning, I had no reason to be concerned. I answered. It was Ty. He didn't sound right.

"We've got a problem," he said. "NASCAR has found something in our fuel."

"Something in our fuel?" I asked him. That didn't make any sense.

"Yeah," Ty said. "They have impounded our car."

"Well, Ty. We'll be needing that car. How long do they plan to keep it?"

Turned out they were thinking "forever."

News like that could be devastating for any team, especially a young race team like ours. I immediately thought the worst. We're cheaters? We're doomed! What am I going to tell Toyota? What am I going to tell NAPA? What are the fans going to think?

Over the years in NASCAR, we've seen some very creative interpretations of the rules. Okay, cheating. But nobody messes with the fuel or the engine. Everyone knows that.

"No way, Ty," I insisted. "This has got to be some kind of mistake. I'm gonna go find Mike Helton and see what's going on."

When I walked into the trailer where the NASCAR president has his office, I could tell immediately he didn't think this was any mistake. Mike has an intimidating presence, and he was focusing it all on me.

"There's something in your fuel we haven't ever seen before," he informed me. "But don't worry, we'll find out what it is."

Worry, my butt! I was scared to death. This could be the end of my team before it officially began.

I had a great relationship with Mike. He was one of Dale's best friends. Mike would go fishing with us sometimes. In the years after Dale's death, Mike was the guy I turned to for advice. Like Dale and I had, Mike and I talked about life, cars, almost anything. As I contemplated my new role as a car owner in the NASCAR world, I sought direction from Mike. I also asked him if he agreed with some of the business decisions I was making. At the same time, being married wasn't going so well for Mrs. Waltrip and me. Mike heard a lot about that as well.

So I asked him as a friend, not as the NASCAR president: "What should I do? You think I should load my car up and get out of here? I love the Daytona 500. I don't want me being here to scar it."

Mike shook his head.

"I don't think you should leave," he said. "You should do what you've done your whole career. Push ahead. You're not a quitter."

It's funny, my dad would have said the same thing in different words. Dad would have told me, "Face the music, son."

"I have to warn you," Mike added as I got up to leave. "If whatever's in your fuel doesn't belong——and I don't think it does——it's going to be expensive."

I could sort of already tell by the way he was acting that that was going to be the case.

Mike didn't say so, but I don't believe he thought I had any knowledge about whatever was wrong with my fuel. That made me feel better.

By the time I left Mike Helton's office, my whole world had been turned upside down. Face the music, you say, Leroy? Well, the music was all cued up and ready to play as soon as I walked out of that trailer. Media types ten folks deep were ready to jump on me.

Fantastic, I thought.

All the people who had been reporting the feel-good story of Michael Waltrip Racing were now focused on us for a much different reason. "What's wrong with your fuel?" they were asking. "Is this a Toyota issue?" Oh, great. Now I've dragged Toyota into this with me.

I'd never been faced with questions like this before, and I didn't have the answers. I didn't know. I told the reporters that as soon as I did know something, I would tell them. As I went to investigate, I thought: How could this be happening to us? Imagine. Even before we started our first race, we managed to alienate our fans. We were labeled cheaters by the media.

Later that week, the analysis came back from NASCAR. They informed us and the whole world our gas had rocket fuel in it. Really? Rocket fuel? How do you even *get* rocket fuel? We were fined $100,000 and had a couple of our key crew members suspended. Our promising start could not have gone more dramatically wrong.

We never found out for sure how it got there. But it is the crew chief's responsibility to make sure the car passes NASCAR's technical inspection. Obviously, with the addition of space-shuttle fuel, that didn't happen.

So there I was again in Daytona without a crew chief. Only this time, in addition to that, NASCAR had taken my car and told me I couldn't practice. That's a lot to be faced with.

After calls to NAPA, Aaron's, Toyota, and all my sponsors, we agreed with Mr. Helton and my dad, Leroy. We had to stay there and push forward. I was going to attempt to qualify my backup car into the 500 without a lap of practice.

I was able to do just that, racing my way through Thursday's qualifying race. But so what? Such damage had been done to me personally that qualifying didn't seem like a big deal. We had worked so hard to help Toyota gain acceptance in NASCAR, and I had invested every dollar I had to build our team. But because of what had happened with our fuel, driving my way into the 500 field hardly mattered to me.

I had gone from proud and happy when I arrived in Daytona to embarrassed and sad. Remember I said I couldn't handle being embarrassed? Well, I was. The only thing people wanted to talk about was what had happened with our fuel. I wanted to do what I had always done when I was hurting. Bury it. Definitely don't talk about it. But I was in Daytona. I couldn't hide there like I do at home.

There was only one reason we survived what could have been that fatal rocket-fuel blow: the relationships I had with my sponsors. NAPA, Aaron's, Coca-Cola, and Best Western had been with me since the Dale days. They knew I wouldn't pull a stunt like that. I'd known the folks from Toyota for only a year or two. But they too had confidence in my integrity.

But we still paid a painful price. Our reputation was harmed. And after that, we had real trouble getting my car back on track. Literally. I left Daytona without a crew chief. And this time, I wasn't driving for the mighty DEI. I was on a new team with a new car. A Toyota. None of the Toyotas were doing very well in their inaugural season either. Our aerodynamics were off, and our engines didn't have the power they needed. Remember the copy machine that was getting on my nerves? The results— or lack of results would be a better way to put it—that it was printing had FAILURE stamped all over them.

The #55 NAPA Toyota did not qualify for another race until Dover that June, missing eleven races in a row. With each DNQ, it got harder and harder to show my face at the track, let alone at the race shop.

But I was the leader. Ty and my boys needed me. And more often than not, I wasn't there.

Even though our sponsors stuck with us, the combination of the cheating scandal and us missing races was putting the financial squeeze on me, the team owner. My name was on the building. I was responsible for the bills. I'd borrowed all my banker, Hondo, could loan me. Ty and my finance guy explained to me in early April that we were in trouble. By the end of September, according to those two, we would be out of money.

The dream was falling apart.

The bank was nervous. And the vendors had begun kindly asking me if I had a plan to catch up my delinquent bills. I didn't one hundred percent have a plan, but I had faith I would figure one out.

This was the kind of pressure I didn't need. No one needed that. It was taking its toll on my personal life. At about that time Buffy and I had decided to separate. I knew the past year or so hadn't been that smooth for us, and I guess the way I handled the start of the 2007 season was more than our relationship could bear. If I had been distant before, after I left Daytona that February I took it to a whole new level.

And if that wasn't enough to deal with, I had a car wreck about that time that could have killed me.

One late night coming from a friend's house, I fell asleep driving on a road near my home. My car flipped over and hit a telephone pole. I was uninjured but again embarrassed. I was only about a quarter mile or so from my house so I just walked home. The next day, I was contacted by the local sheriff about my accident. I explained to him it was late, there was no one around, and I just wanted to go home. And that's what I did. I didn't realize I had done anything wrong by leaving. Was I supposed to just sit there? Turns out, yes. There's not a lot of traffic in Sherrills Ford at that time of night. Just sitting there didn't occur to me.

So let's summarize what was going on in my life at that point. My wife had left. I had a scary car wreck that made people question what I was doing out at that time of night. And then there was the minor detail of my financial situation. Everything I'd worked for my whole life was going down the drain because of my team's inability to perform competitively.

People love to talk. And in the weeks and months that followed, they talked. But one thing I was thankful for: No one was talking about me and Buffy. She and I loved each other. We just found it harder and harder to live together. Our main focus was to make sure our beautiful daughter, Macy, knew we both loved her. So Buffy and I were nice to each other, and we always will be.

So I found myself in another quite difficult situation. Again, it was time to make some serious decisions. I never seem to go too long without moments like these. I was starting to learn from experience. I was figuring out what worked for me and what didn't. It never seemed to happen quickly enough, but eventually I learned.

One thing I was quite confident about: There was only one person capable of pulling me out of where I was. That person was me. I'd had help with this twice before, when Dale got me going. One time, it was his idea, the you-will-win-in-my-car speech. The other time it was mine, because I didn't want to let him down. And now, it was time to call on Big E for some of that help again.

Things weren't going well for me. I didn't like who I was or where I was. I made a decision. I was tired of sitting idly by.

I was home one evening all by myself. No Buffy. No Macy. I didn't even have a dog. But I had a mirror, and I looked in that mirror. It made me look way deeper than the reflection I saw. I looked down inside myself. I thought about how Dale had taken a guy who had never won a race before and convinced him that he couldn't lose. And when that guy needed to rescue his season, Dale had been there again.

Dale guided me in that direction, but I was the one who had to believe what he said. I couldn't just go do it because Dale said I could. I had to believe I could. He had given me the coaching I needed. He pointed me there. But I had to take the journey for myself. And take it I did.

When it was time to snap my losing streak, when it was time to reclaim my season, whatever the challenge was, my motivation came from Dale. I felt like I was letting him down again and that was not acceptable.

There was no way I would just allow this team to fail, this team I had worked so hard for and was so proud of. As I sat at home that night, I knew I had to get more involved. I had to go help the people I had hired. I had to get back in there and rally my troops around me.

Why had it taken so long to make that brilliant decision? Why did I keep needing to learn, over and over again? I don't have a great answer for that. But once I decided, I was determined to see my decision through.

Before Dale became part of my life, I had to survive, but surviving was all I was doing. My survival on the track led me to Dale's car and the winner's circle. In the middle of 2007, my survival was in question again. I needed something almost magical to happen, according to my financial advisors. All my money, everything I had invested in building Michael Waltrip Racing was in serious jeopardy. We were a couple of months away from the bank owning the whole joint. No one wanted that. Especially me.

I needed something extraordinary to happen. It happened before— actually twice, down in Daytona. And I needed it to happen again. The word was out on the NASCAR street: "Michael is in trouble. He won't be able to pay his bills much longer." The sharks were circling. What do I do? What would Dale do? Who could I turn to?

You might be surprised.

I called the soon-to-be-former Mrs. Waltrip. I told her: "I want to talk."

Finally.

Those were four words that Private Mike rarely used. Unlike Public

Mike, Private Mike ain't a talker. But I had some things I needed to say. I wanted her to know I was sorry for letting our marriage slip away. Sorry for trying to deal with all the drama in my life by simply burying it, hoping it would go away. That was certainly no way to maintain a healthy partnership between a husband and wife. That sounds like stuff you'd discover about yourself lying on a couch in some doctor's office, doesn't it? I'm friends with Dr. Phil. But I've never been on his couch. I do watch his show a lot. Maybe that helped me figure some things out.

After my confession to Buffy on the personal side, it was time to talk business. I explained to her that the team was in dire straits financially.

I told her I was having trouble paying for all the stuff I'd bought, even that damn copy machine. She already knew there were issues, but she didn't know how serious they were. We needed to put our heads together and come up with a plan. We needed to call someone—anyone!—and see if they wanted to own a race team.

Buffy had an idea. She called a friend, who called a friend. Then she called me back and said, "Johnny knows a man you need to meet."

Johnny was Johnny Harris, a Charlotte businessman with connections all over the world. Johnny had a friend named Rob who loved racing. That Rob was Rob Kauffman.

Rob came to Charlotte from London in May 2007. We spent a couple of days talking about how a partnership between us might work. Rob headed back to London and said he would get back to me in a couple of weeks. We began organizing our partnership. By October of that year, he was 50 percent owner of Michael Waltrip Racing.

Rob is a billionaire and I was in trouble. Don't tell anybody, about the bind I was in, Okay? He could have taken all of MWR if he wanted, and it would be known today as RKR. But Rob is not that kind of guy. He appreciated what I had built, and he wanted us to be partners. Every time I tell this story, it makes me cry. I can't imagine not having the team I love so much, and I would have lost it if it weren't for Rob Kauffman. With Rob's support and partnership, we began making steady progress, going from missing races to making all of them to winning our first race in Charlotte in 2009. That was the same race where I began my Cup career as a driver twenty-four years earlier.

A Cup win didn't seem so likely when I was sitting in Mike Helton's office in 2007 talking about stupid fuel additives that had the capability of shooting you into space. Nor did it seem likely before I met Rob in the middle of the same year.

The trophy we won in Charlotte, my first as a car owner, has a prominent position in our shop. If you come to Cornelius, North Carolina, you can see it yourself. I walk past that trophy regularly. And when I do, it reminds me of the little old lady on that bus back in Kentucky. "Rejoice in the moment," she said. "Enjoy your victory. Don't take what you've accomplished for granted." What great advice that turned out to be!

That trophy represents a lot to me. It reminds me what a long road I've driven to get where I am today. From a young racer who didn't think he could lose to a guy who wondered if he'd ever win.

As a kid, race cars and high-banked turns inspired me. They were all I thought about. They brought me closer to my dad. They focused my dreams. They drove me. But as the years rolled by—and the miles—I came to see that it was always the people who mattered most. The ones who helped me buy tires and cars and parts and pieces. The ones who cheered me on. The ones who made me want to win. I couldn't have had success in racing without them. Bobby, Darrell, Richard, Dick, and so many others. But one guy defined me—and continues to do so—both professionally and personally. His direction made me a winner. He's never stopped guiding me.

Glad you're still with me, Dale.